From Brooklyn
to Tokyo Bay

FROM BROOKLYN
TO
TOKYO BAY

A Sailor's Story
of WWII

Albert R. Pincus

Turner Publishing Company
Paducah, Kentucky

Turner®
PUBLISHING COMPANY

412 Broadway • P.O. Box 3101
Paducah, Kentucky 42002-3101
(270) 443-0121
www.turnerpublishing.com

Turner Publishing Company Staff:
Eddie Sheridan, Editor
Shelley R. Davidson, Designer

Library of Congress Control No: 2003115161

ISBN 978-1-68162-229-3

Printed in the United States of America

RRH   0   9   8   7   6   5   4   3   2   1

Contents

Acknowledgments

Since joining the LSM/LSMR/Association, I have been privileged to find some of my old shipmates, as well as some who have since gone to their reward. I am proud to mention those I remember along with some of the adventures we had as a crew sailing a new and untried type of ship to the war zone where some of the fiercest fighting was taking place. I have had much correspondence with those I was able to find and with the shipmates living in the state of Pennsylvania. I have had reunions, and I continue to meet with one of them, MM2/c Warren Robertson. We have managed to keep those memories alive, exchanging pictures and stories. It is a privilege to be able to write about Warren, Josh Cope, Dr. Wilbur Helmerich, Bill Cooley, Richard Hoch, Jim Bjelland, Ed Rhodes, Paul Stevens, and Jerry Cannon, all of whom served with me aboard the LSM-472, and with whom I have either met or exchanged correspondence with in the past year. It was wonderful to find them and be in contact again after so many years.

I thank them for the information they gave me, for refreshing my memory, and, most of all, for remembering me.

I also acknowledge, with love, the help of my daughter, Elizabeth Libutti, who put my notes together and corrected my spelling and prepared the final draft of this saga. I will always see the tears in her eyes as she read all about her father and his young shipmates with whom he took this "Perilous Journey."

From Brooklyn to Tokyo Bay

Foreword

Throughout history, the United States has seen many conflagrations, from its own War for Independence to the so-called police actions in Korea and Vietnam. The Second World War, however, seems to stand out as one of the fiercest and most frightening of all, perhaps because our own liberty and freedom, so long enjoyed, was at stake. It was a war to save our Democracy for ourselves and our future generations. In no other war, except for the Revolution, was our own liberty at stake, and the Revolution was at a time when the concept of our Democracy was quite new. Many heroes, like George Washington, were fighting against their own people, so to speak, in the Revolution. It must have been difficult for those colonial minute men to fight their own kind, but they realized it had to be done in order to establish a new Democratic form of government unlike anything the world had seen prior to our Declaration of Independence. So it was that our young men and women, polarized by the attack on Pearl Harbor and the threat to our very existence, suddenly became as one and fought the enemy back to its own shores and its ultimate surrender. The important fact was that this war was in great part fought with young men, mostly teenagers, along-side the seasoned military, and they literally grew to manhood amidst the horrors of war.

This is the story of one such young man of 18, who left high school to volunteer for the Navy, and it chronicles his life aboard two naval ships, both of which have since joined others like them in the scrap heap. It is, therefore, fitting that such an interesting tale be told while some of the survivors of that war are still with us, so that their descendants will know not only who they were and what they accomplished in those dark days, but also that the freedom which they enjoy today was paid for in blood yesterday. While I was too young for the military at that time, I am privileged to know this author and my own father, who served as well. I, therefore, recommend this interesting story of a very young teenager who took a perilous journey from the streets of Brooklyn, New York, to the shores of the enemy in Japan, and who, fortunately, lived to tell about it.

Lt. General Frank Libutti
United States Marine Corps, (Retired)

Introduction

"December 7, 1941, a day that will live in infamy," began for we northeasterners like all the other cold and bleak December mornings in our part of the world, in this case, Brooklyn, New York. Usually, Sundays during winter were quiet, cold, and more or less peaceful in Bensonhurst. But this morning was quite different from the usual, because of the cowardly early morning attack on Pearl Harbor, Hawaii.

The devastation and chaos were almost unimaginable to us, on the other side of the globe, and the sadness at the loss of our Navy and all of those military forces soon turned to hatred toward our enemy. As far as the average American citizen was concerned, it was not only unbelievable, but totally unacceptable, and in those few hours, the entire country was suddenly turned into a group with only one purpose — to avenge our military and destroy our common enemy. Immediately, our armed forces were bulging with new recruits anxious to do their part in the war effort and to get into the fight.

I doubt that anywhere in recent history can you find another example of unity of purpose and dedication to the cause than in those dark days of December 1941.

The entire country became as one, from the military to "Rosie the Riveter" on the home front, and the giants of industry – auto makers, shipbuilders, and even clothing manufacturers – all altered their normal routines and became part of the war effort. It was, in a sad way, a reminder of what a free and Democratic nation can accomplish when faced with the possibility of losing its liberty.

My buddies and I were proud to be a part of this new America, which was gearing up for the greatest war and danger it had ever faced. No one complained about rationing, no new cars or appliances. Instead they became as one with one purpose — to defeat the enemy and send him back to the land of the rising sun.

The following story documents the travels and experiences of one young man who went through a metamorphosis from boyhood to manhood during the fierce and frightening years of WWII. There are thousands of such stories that will shortly be forgotten, as were the ships that made up that wonderful new Navy 60 years ago. As the young men and women who served their country and made it safe once again for democracy leave this world, as all of us must, it seems important that some of them document their own stories of the war and their adventures, so that their own descendants, as well as total strangers of the coming generations, will have an account of those happenings which shaped the new world and made it possible for those future generations to enjoy the freedom they have and be aware that those freedoms were what these men and women helped to preserve.

The history books used in our schools today, I understand, only devote a few pages to WWII. That conflagration deserves much more, and it is for that reason that this book and so many more like it have been written. The intent is not only to honor the memory of those who gave the supreme sacrifice, those who still suffer from wounds and the rest who were fortunate enough, like myself, to have survived intact, but to alert the new generation to the fact that Democracy is not free and that it took a great deal of American blood to keep it. They must not only appreciate what happened so many years ago, but more important, they must be vigilant and ready to do the same if our country is threatened once again.

We who were fortunate enough to return are not heroes, but survivors. The real heroes remain overseas, where they fell in defense of this great country.

Chapter One
Pinky's Candy Store

___

T he special lunch for teenagers attending
Lafayette High School, near famed Coney
Island, was a three-cent chocolate egg cream
(milk first, of course, in true Brooklyn style), a one-
cent pretzel log, and, for dessert, a loose cigarette (your
choice of 20 Grand or Wings). This sumptuous repast
could only be purchased at Pinky's Candy Store on
West 8th Street and Avenue O, next to the Sea Beach
train station, in Brooklyn, and it was served up by
Sarah "Momma" Pincus, while Izzy Pincus put a couple
of slugs into the aging jukebox and played a Glenn
Miller or Benny Goodman tune. Izzy knew what the
boys liked and what they played in their cellar club on
social nights, and he and Sarah were considered sur-
rogate parents. Pinky's was a home away from home,
where Momma's boys could dance or do some last
minute homework in one of the booths. Sarah and Izzy's
son, Albert, known in those days as "Pinky," was a
member of the cellar club, Club Cherokee, and the
hero of the club was Charlie Barnett and his orches-
tra. On the first of every month, there was a flurry of
activity by the boys to get together the rent for the
cellar club, which was $13.00, a huge sum in 1940.

Many times when they were short a buck or two, Momma Pincus would kick in the difference and warn them not to tell Izzy, but he knew it all along and said nothing because these boys were like his own children. He enjoyed them hanging around, being helpful with folding the Sunday newspapers, and he especially loved the way they danced the Lindy Hop with the neighborhood girls. In those difficult days after the Great Depression, in which Izzy had lost his fleet of taxi cabs and all his assets, running the candy store, watching these nice kids grow up and enjoying the big band music while seeing those kids happily dancing made up in great part for the financial loss he had endured.

Pinky's Candy Store at West 8th Street and Avenue O, at the Seabeach Express Subway Station in the fall of 1941, just prior to the attack on Pearl Harbor.

Sarah "Momma" Pincus, Izzy Pincus, and Sonny Siegel, one of the regular gang always present in the store. Notice the treats of yesteryear on the counter – penny candy, chocolate covered jellies, and nuts, as well as charlotte Russe on the right of the counter at 5 cents each. Pinky's featured Breyers Ice Cream and Fox's U-Bet Syrups. Both companies are still in business.

A distant cousin, Ralph, was employed by the juke-box company, and he always saw to it that the newest and best records were placed weekly in the big Wurlitzer. He always gave Izzy a handful of slugs so he could make it play free for the kids. So life was okay, although Momma and Izzy worked very hard and long hours, opening at 5:30 a.m. every morning except Monday to catch the newspaper crowd getting on the subway to go to work.

They did not close every night until midnight, and on Saturday nights they stayed open until 3:00 a.m. sometimes just so the kids would have a place to meet and talk a little after date night, have an egg cream and a loose cigarette before going home. On Wednesday nights, the kids could be found at the high school with their respective club team playing a basketball game or practicing for one. If the school was not available, they were permitted to use the court at the local Jewish Community Center on Bay Parkway. The two best teams were the Trylons, named for the 1939 World's Fair symbol, and the Elroys. Pinky was a member of the Trylons, but the boys in those two clubs were Izzy and Momma's boys, and after a game they would gather at Pinky's to talk about the game. Izzy would, as usual, drop some of Ralph's slugs into the jukebox, and Momma would say to him how much she liked those kids and always tried to keep them out of trouble. They felt at ease talking to her about everything from school problems to girl problems, and she always gave good, sound advice. Even though Izzy was more stern, beyond his tough facade, Momma knew he loved all those boys, especially his own youngest child, Albert, better known as "Pinky," who was one of them.

On the morning of December 7, 1941, "a day that will live in infamy," Izzy and Pinky had been busy since

5:30 a.m. folding the Sunday papers and getting the store ready for a busy winter morning when Izzy expected everyone from Christmas shoppers to the Trylons and Elroys to show up. As usual, when Pinky was not in school, he helped in the store by making sodas and other fountain desserts that delighted patrons. He and Izzy could make the best egg cream in Brooklyn, with milk first, of course, since that and holding the glass on its side as you filled it was the secret to making a foamy head that was their symbol and made for the tastiest creation. As the morning wore on and customers came and went, things seemed to be going smoothly for Pinky and Izzy, when suddenly, at approximately 12:30 p.m., the radio, which was playing Glenn Miller tunes, was interrupted by a bulletin. A huge armada of ships and aircraft belonging to the Imperial Japanese Navy had attacked Pearl Harbor and practically wiped out most of the U.S. Navy fleet stationed there. They were caught by surprise and totally devastated. The mighty battleship, the *Arizona*, was already in its watery grave, where it still rests today, a monument to the sailors and marines who died with her, never even knowing what really had happened so suddenly that fateful morning.

Pinky and Izzy were stunned, then angered. How could this have happened and why? That afternoon, the candy store was filled with the Trylons, the Elroys, and their girlfriends, all of whom were 17 and 18 years of age. We all knew that this could be a war to the death and that each one of us would be affected. We knew what we had to do, and that was to defend our country at all costs. When I reflect on those days now, so many years later, I cannot help but think of the members we lost to war. Berney Smith and Joey Schildkraut of the Elroys, both killed at the Battle of the Bulge, and so many more, plucked from a wonderful life at such an early age. There was a lot of crying and hugging at the store that day, and later the rest of Sarah and Izzy's family arrived to talk about it and try to reason it out. Of course, all the boys wanted to join the armed forces immediately, but Momma said they should calm down and go home and talk to their parents before doing anything rash. They all agreed, but you could see in their faces that they were going to fight for their country no matter what.

It was hard to understand what had happened, especially since the Japanese ambassador had met with President Roosevelt just a few days before the attack to work out certain differences. It was clear to all that the Japanese must have planned the attack and trained for it for many months prior. So the meetings were a sham, while the Japanese got ready to destroy our navy.

Unfortunately, all or most of our battleships were at Pearl Harbor, and, due to some serious mistakes by some of our people, early warnings went unheeded. As a result, all of those ships were sunk or severely damaged, and, more importantly, many who manned those ships were lost as well. The *Arizona* alone took over two-thousand men to a watery grave, where they still remain to this day, a monument to their heroism on that day of infamy.

Fortunately, that war and all wars that came after it were fought with aircraft carriers and amphibious ships, such as my own Landing Ship Medium 472. Our aircraft carriers on December 7, 1941, were deployed elsewhere, and the new amphibious force had not yet been initiated. So we were able to strike back eventually with carrier based planes while the battleships were repaired. As many as six hundred Destroyer

Escorts were built to protect those large ships, as well as to sink the Japanese and Nazi submarines which were trying to destroy our ships.

It was indeed strange that the Japanese Ambassador was told to deliver the Japanese Declaration of War at precisely 1:00 p.m., Eastern Standard Time, to Secretary Cordell Hull. It was, of course, planned that the attack on Pearl Harbor would have already taken place at 7:00 a.m., Honolulu time. The entire operation was planned that way. Although America was devastated, I still remember those somber words spoken by Admiral Yamamoto of the Imperial Japanese Navy: "I am afraid we have awakened a sleeping giant." He could not have been more correct.

Liberty in Acapulco, Mexico. Sparks is on shore patrol in the local brothel, surrounded by his shipmates.

Above: Three Brooklyn wise guys on leave – Artie, Alan, and me, in the center, after the war. Alan became my law partner.

Left: Sparky leaves the ship to go on shore patrol duty at Wakanoura, Japan.

Chapter Two

The U.S. Navy Gets Three Anxious Apprentice Seamen

The war was not going too well in those early days. Corregidor had fallen. General Douglas MacArthur had to leave by way of a P.T. boat in total defeat, and he made that fateful statement, "I will return." As he left, the rest of the American soldiers were shortly thereafter forced to commence the death march from which many did not return.

My two best friends and I, Whitey Robbins of the Elroys and Willy Levine, who lived opposite Pinky's Candy Store, were on our way to Lafayette High School, where we were all seniors. We looked at each other and, without a spoken word, we all knew what we had to do. So we cut school and headed for the Army Air Corps, because, as Whitey said, they had the best looking uniforms, and, besides, Willy was an airplane nut who always wanted to fly. He would go down to Floyd Bennett field every weekend to watch the small planes take off and land and would try to bum a ride, which he did at times. We all passed the physical, except that Whitey and I both had poor depth perception. The army doctor said it was a shame because we were good physical specimens, but if we tried to land a plane, the chances were we would crash. As for Willy, he had a slight cross-eye, which disqualified him. He was particularly disappointed, but the doctor told him to exercise by holding a pencil in front of him and slowly bringing it to his forehead and between his eyes, and that would be a good exercise to strengthen his weak eye muscle. For almost four years, Willy did just that, and, ultimately, it must have worked, because when we all got out of the service, Willy was so determined to fly that he volunteered for the Israeli Air Force and became a fighter pilot with many victories to his credit. He later became a decorated colonel in the fledgling air force, married an Israeli girl, and never returned to the USA. We never saw him again.

Meanwhile, back at WWII, we all decided that the next best service was the Navy, and we were pleased that we passed with flying colors and became apprentice seamen in the greatest navy the world had ever seen or will ever see. We left for boot camp at Great Lakes Naval Training Station in Illinois after tearful good-byes and a big party at Club Cherokee. Momma and Izzy were not too happy, since it would have been some time before we were drafted and, besides, we did not even get our diplomas and graduate. But there was no question that they and everyone else at Pinky's were all very proud of us.

And so it was that I traded my beautiful blue satin club jacket with the Trylon emblem on one sleeve and my number 22 on the other for Navy blues, a definite change from a teenager to an adult as a member of the greatest Navy the world had ever known. We were a bunch of citizen sailors anxious to protect and defend our country, and so our long journey, which lasted almost four years, had begun.

Boot camp was no bed of roses, and we were worked hard and fast because the Navy needed more and more of the citizen sailors to man the ships of war, which were being built in record numbers. A lot of the work on those ships was being done by the girls who were affectionately known as "Rosie the Riveter." Great Lakes was cold, damp, and unfriendly and was our first taste of the military, as well as the first time any of us was ever away from home. Brooklyn was far away, and we really were on our own for the first time. As for myself, I had never been outside of New York, except to Lake Hopatcong, New Jersey, where my sister, Ethel, and her husband, William, had a summer retreat that they rented. On one other occasion, before leaving for the Navy, I had volunteered to pick apples in upstate New York and was excused from school for three weeks to do just that, because there was not enough manpower to pick the apples, which started to rot on the trees. We lived in a camp, and I don't know which was worse, but I can say that the Navy was cleaner. After marching, exercising, and instructions from the Blue Jackets manual learning to speak Navy and make all kinds of knots, most of which I have now forgotten from years of non-use, we were given aptitude tests. It was determined that I would be a good electrician's mate, and so, after my leave, both Whitey and I were assigned to Electrician's Mate School at Purdue University in Lafayette, Indiana, a beautiful campus where we learned electrical engineering.

On my first leave after boot camp, and before reporting to Purdue University to study to be an electrician's mate, I had a wonderful time back in Brooklyn. Of course, as always, Pinky's Candy Store was the meeting place. The folks were happy to have me home for a short time, and my older brother, Harry, loaned me his car a few times. It was a 1941 Packard 120 convertible, black with tan upholstery and a tan

Home on leave from the submarine base at Kodiak Island, Alaska. The car was my older brother's 1941 Packard 120 convertible, parked in front of Pinky's Candy Store.

top. It was a beauty, and Harry was very proud of it, especially now that no more cars were being made and all the car companies were making war machines.

On one occasion, I borrowed the car and all of my friends and I took a drive to Long Beach because it was such a beautiful day. The route took us over the causeway, which had a tollbooth with a ten-cent toll. This was the same tollbooth used in the first *Godfather* movie, where actor James Caan, who portrayed mobster Sonny Corleone, was gunned down in his fancy Lincoln automobile. As we approached the booth, I asked my friends if anyone had a dime, as I had no change. One of the boys said I did not have to pay since I was in uniform, but instead had to give the toll

collector a victory sign by showing my two fingers forming a V and motioning up and down three times. I replied, "Since when is that the rule?" and their reply
was that it was new and just for GIs coming home on
leave. I slowed down as I approached the tollbooth,
and when the toll collector stuck out his hand, I smiled
and made the sign and motioned three times as instructed
by my buddies and then proceeded through the booth.
No sooner had we cleared the booth then we were pulled
over by a motorcycle cop, who said, "Hey, sailor, what
are you, a wise guy? Why didn't you pay the toll?" I replied, "I don't have to pay because I am in uniform, and
my friends just told me about the new law for service-
men." All my buddies broke into hysterical laughter. I
turned red as a beet as I stuttered an apology, but the
cop started to laugh as well and said, "Go on sailor, I'll
pay the toll for you." Those were the kind of pranks we
Club Cherokee boys used to play on one another. I
guess, in retrospect, both Sonny Corleone and myself
got into trouble for not paying that toll!

*Myself and two shipmates, Nat Kurtz and Steve Cardia, on Pyra-
mid Mountain, Kodiak, Alaska.*

The author on shore patrol at Nagoya, Japan.

Chapter Three

The U.S. Navy Submarine Base
Kodiak Island, Alaska

G raduation from Purdue University was nothing to write home about, but I must admit it was interesting to learn about electricity. The best thing I remember about that time was the night that Stan Kenton and his band came to perform for us. He was one of my favorites, and I owned copies of all his records. I was first in line at the huge auditorium on campus, having skipped dinner so I would be sure to get a front-row seat. The place was soon packed, and, suddenly, there was my hero. He was well over six feet tall, with his well-known crew cut blond hair and his big smile.

He played all of my favorite tunes, and I could close my eyes and imagine I was back in Brooklyn at Club Cherokee on a social night. After his last selection, he asked if one of the sailors in the audience would like to lead his band. Every hand went up, and I was stunned when he looked down at me and said, "You, sailor, come up and lead my band." As he handed me his baton, he said, "What would you like them to play?" I replied, "Why, *Eager Beaver*, of course." That was his great theme song. "Good choice," he replied, and there I was, leading one of the greatest swing bands of the time. I have never forgotten that wonderful experience. Stan is gone to the big band in the sky now, but whenever I play one of his old records, which I have kept in my collection all these years, I am transported once again to Thatcher Hall and I am eighteen years old and in all my glory, leading my hero's band.

The worst memory I have of that great school is the night I was coming back from my liberty. I had a date with a lovely blonde, and her twin sister was dating Whitey. We agreed that since it was late, Whitey would go back and I would drop off the girls at their home and take a taxi back to the base. Liberty was almost over, and in a few moments I would be AWOL and on report and lose my next liberty. So, as the cab came up to the base, I could not wait and stepped out while he was moving at about thirty miles per hour. I rolled over and over and slid to a halt at the gatehouse and just made it, but I was sore all over and had a big hole in my white pants, which had literally fallen apart as I slid. In baseball, men slide from third base to home plate, but for me the slide was from a taxi to our officer of the day, safe at home plate on time.

After graduation, we were promoted to firemen 1st class and were given our anxiously awaited assignments. We received our assignments, and we were upset that we all were going in different directions. I never saw Whitey and Willy again until after the war, and I was assigned to the Navy submarine base at Kodiak Island, Alaska. We had a somber goodbye, as we embraced each other and promised to meet again if we survived the war.

The flight to Kodiak, the first and largest island in the Aleutian chain, in an old DC-3 prop plane was very rough, and the island was even worse. It was the dark half of the year, and with the ban on all lights, blackened windows, and half-covered headlights on the few cars on the island, it was pretty bleak. The base had only three ships, two WWI destroyers, the *Hatfield* and the *Fox,* and one WWI submarine, and a bunch of green kids to man them. In the meantime, the Japanese had taken Attu and Kiska and were very close. They did not attack because they were not sure what we had, and they knew there was an army garrison on our island as well. We would have been a pushover for them, but we were lucky, and, subsequently, our forces took back those two islands. It was the ill-fated cruiser *Indianapolis* that led the invasion. That wonderful ship was sunk by a Japanese sub in the closing days of the war after delivering the atom bomb to the base from which it would be flown to and dropped on Hiroshima. The ship went down after two torpedo hits and after its powder magazine blew up. Of the crew of 1,100 men and officers, about eight-hundred survived and floated helplessly in the icy shark-infested waters, and when they were finally rescued, five days later, only three-hundred-and-eighty were left. Captain McVey, commanding officer, was court-martialed for failing to zigzag in enemy waters, but it later came out that he was not to blame, as confirmed by the commanding office of the Japanese sub. Nevertheless, he was demoted and later committed suicide.

Meanwhile, back on Kodiak Island, I had been promoted to fireman 1/c and was taking my turn at KP duty in the galley peeling potatoes. The chief cook, an old timer with twenty years service, asked if anyone could drive a pickup truck to get off KP duty. We were all kids, and no one had a driver's license, but I could drive, since I loved cars and always sat in the family car and shifted, pretending to be actually driving. I was the only one who raised my hand, but all the others raised their eyebrows, wondering if I was lying just to get off KP duty. Cooky, as the chief was called, took me out back of the mess hall and showed me his pride; a 1937 red Chevy closed pickup truck, which had obviously seen better days. But he was proud of it because it was one of only a very few non-military vehicles on the island. He told me he had baked forty-eight pies for the army garrison, and we proceeded to load them into pie racks and then load the two huge racks into the truck. Cooky then said I was to take them to the army garrison, and he gave me a map on a crumpled piece of paper, since there were no roads or road signs or anything but total blackness. I started out gritting gears as I went down the so-called road, following the homemade map. It struck me that Cooky was a lot better at cooking than map making, and he wasn't such a great cook to begin with!

It was bitter cold on Kodiak Island in the dead of winter, and I strained my eyes trying to make out the landmarks on Cooky's map. After a while, I was hopelessly lost. Never having had a good sense of direction all my young life, I was not at all surprised to be lost on this God forsaken island in the pitch black and cold of a brutal winter in the middle of a war. I decided I had better backtrack a little and look for one of the landmarks. As I turned the old wagon around to get back to the way I had come, I was surprised to find the truck leaning over to one side, and one of the rear wheels seemed not to be on the road. I pulled up the emergency brake and got out to look around and was horrified to find that the truck was on a hill or mountain, and the left rear wheel was off the road, hanging over a sheer drop. I froze, and then I figured out that the only way to get back on the road was to give her the gas and pray. I did just that and floored the accelerator. The old girl moaned and jumped back on the road, but my elation was short-lived because the two pie racks hit the rear doors of the old panel truck, which opened from the force of the blow. Out came the two racks laden with wonderful pies, each of which went flying off that mountain like forty-eight great Frisbees sailing quickly down to heaven only knows where. I was stunned and could not believe what had just happened. Of course, I was afraid that this was the end of my naval career and I would end up in the brig. I finally found my way back to the base, and there was Cooky, who asked how everything went. My reply was, "Cooky, can we talk?" I thereupon told him of my misadventure. Much to my surprise, he laughed. "It serves those dog faces right. Let them bake their own pies," he said. He then said that if I wanted to be forgiven, I would have to donate a package that had just arrived in the mail for me. He said it was salami, because he smelled it minutes before the mail truck arrived with it. Sure enough, it was salami from my mom, which had taken six weeks to reach me from the fleet post office (without refrigeration). I said to throw it out, but Cooky merely washed all the green mold right off with hot water, peeled the skin off and then sliced it and made powdered eggs and salami for all the mess hall crew, a delicacy we had not had in months. Cooky said as we ate, "Too bad it didn't take a couple of more weeks, it would have tasted even better." So from a defeat came a victory, and I was off KP duty for good!

After a few months of this horrible duty, I was finally transferred to a brand new ship just completed in Charleston, South Carolina, the *USS Chaffee,* a Destroyer Escort Number 230. She was a beauty, with all the latest bells and whistles. A steam turbo electric vessel about 300 feet long with a five inch gun turret forward and aft and numerous anti-aircraft guns, 50 cal. machine guns, and a great many depth charges and Y guns for use against enemy submarines. We had been taking an awful beating at the hands of both the Nazis and the Japanese subs, and this was our Navy's answer to that threat. At one point, the Navy had over six hundred of these fabulous sub-hunters. They were fast and extremely maneuverable, with underwater sonar equipment to track and destroy subs with depth charges called ash cans. They simply rolled off the fantail of the ship when a sub was detected or when shot outward by the ship's Y-guns. This was a new kind of fighting ship, and we were all very proud of her. I was promoted to electrician's mate 3/c, and, along with another electrician, Sal Amico from the Bronx, was put in charge of maintaining the generators and the electrical switchboard. We took the ship to Bermuda for a shakedown cruise, and all went well, except that while the gunner's mates were practicing hitting a moving target, they were so bad that they almost hit the plane towing the target. It was agreed that they needed more practice after the pilot dropped the target and took off, lest he become a target and get shot down as well. We also had the dubious honor of bringing back a German torpedo which had not exploded, so it could be examined by our navy experts.

On the way back from our shakedown cruise to lovely Bermuda, we were all alone in the vast Atlantic Ocean. It was a beautiful clear day, and, frankly, all of us fledgling sailors were actually enjoying this easy cruise when, suddenly, the sonar operator reported to the officers on the bridge that there was a contact and it was something moving toward the *Chaffee*. His guess was that it was a submarine, most likely a Nazi U-boat, of which there were many in these waters. In fact, the new class of small, fast destroyers (called

Destroyer Escorts, of which the *Chaffee* was one) was invented specifically for sub chasing. They were smaller than a destroyer and faster, as well as more maneuverable, and they could be built faster and at less cost than a regular destroyer. These wonderful little ships actually turned the tide in the Atlantic, and the Nazis realized eventually that it was too costly in men and boats to patrol the U.S. coast attempting to sink troop ships as well as supply ships.

Back on the *Chaffee*, the captain sounded general quarters, and we all rushed to our battle stations, ready for action. The captain turned the fast little warship around and headed in the direction that the sonar man had indicated. At full-speed ahead, all depth charges and Y-guns were made ready and the pleasant cruise just moments before was transformed into a warship girding for battle.

"Now hear this!" blared the intercom. "All hands man your battle stations! Prepare to drop depth charges!" "My God," I thought, "we really are at war, and this will be the first test for our new D.E. and its green crew."

The depth charges rolled off the transom of the ship like so many ash cans (as they were called), all primed to explode at different depths. The Y-guns shot additional depth charges further out on each side of the ship. The explosions came steadily, several at a time, and the concussion sent geysers of water up from the surface of the ocean, which even caused our ship to rock and roll as we chased the sub. Eventually, it was over. The sonar lost contact, and it was clear we either sunk the U-boat or it escaped from us. It was our first action at sea, and we were all just a little unnerved by it.

The *Chaffee* then continued on course for New London, Connecticut, where we were to practice with the

U.S. submarines before heading for the Panama Canal and out into the vast Pacific Ocean to join Compac and become part of the force heading east toward the Philippine Islands. To this day, I still wonder if we sunk that sub. But we will never know, because there was no confirmation of a sinking ever received.

The ship was ordered to the submarine base at New London, Connecticut, and we took part in practicing anti-submarine warfare. We became quite proficient in tracking submarines with radar and sonar, both of which were relatively new, but were state of the art for 1943. We became expert at dropping depth charges (ash cans) and using the Y-guns, and, finally, we were ready. The majestic *Chaffee* steamed out of New London and headed for the Panama Canal and the action in the islands of the South Pacific.

Chapter Four

Life Aboard the
USS *Chaffee* (DE-230)

We navigated the Panama Canal and headed out into the Pacific. We joined up with a fleet of ships and proceeded from one island to the next as picket boat for the protection of the larger naval vessels, as well as the troop ships and the cargo vessels. I made some good friends, whom I still remember: Gordon F. Docherty, motor machinist mate from Boston, Massachusetts, and Claremont Dalton Smith of Baton Rouge, Louisiana, also an electrician's mate, whose first words when he came aboard were, "Anyone who calls me Claremont Dalton will get a mouth full of teeth. My name is C.D. Smith." But my best friend, by far, was Sal Amico. We could understand each other and were very much alike, having both been from New York.

One rainy and rough day, Sal was topside giving up his breakfast to the wild sea, as he did most every morning. He was the most seasick sailor I had ever met. He always had a tube of toothpaste and a brush in his pocket so he could clean up after a bout with seasickness. On this particular morning, he was very sick and finally came down to his station in the engine room, where he and I would parallel the generators and shut down the one that had been on to service it. The other generator would then take over the task of providing electricity for the ship. Sal was wet to his skin that morning, and as we stood on the metal deck plates in front of the electrical switchboard, we each grabbed the switches to parallel the generators, and, presto, he was grounded to the deck plate and the switchboard because he was so wet. We all know that water is a great conductor of electricity. He was frozen and could not let go. In thirty seconds, he would have been electrocuted. I remembered what they had taught us at Purdue. Do not touch him or you too will become grounded. You must tackle him to get him off the equipment, and that is exactly what I did. He was okay, but badly shaken, and, needless to say, he never went near the switchboard while wet ever again.

Sal was so seasick that the ship's pharmacist suggested he be given shore duty. We all said goodbye to him, as we thought we would probably never see each other again. Fate, however, decreed otherwise, and we were destined to meet again more than once during the war and later in civilian life. In the meantime, life aboard the *Chaffee* was fast and furious, as we visited all of those romantic islands you have read about in history books and other accounts of the war in the Pacific. We came upon some of those islands while the invasion was still in progress, and in others we were lucky enough to arrive after the initial battle and while the fighting had gone inland into the jungle. Over a considerable time, as the U.S. forces advanced slowly and at great cost in young soldiers and marines, as well as sailors, we dropped anchor at the Mariannas Islands, the Marshalls, which was the site of not only one of the fiercest battles, but the one that turned the tide in favor of our forces. Then there was Eniwetok,

Guam, Saipan, Tinian, Samar, Naha, Buckner Bay, Tacloban Manicani, and many more, until we finally arrived at Leyte and Luzon in the Philippine Islands, where we took part in the battle of Lingayan Gulf. This was a fierce battle involving many of our ships, which included seventy destroyer escort vessels of the same class as the *Chaffee*. We were part of the escort to protect the *USS Pennsylvania,* a huge and majestic battleship that had to be protected at all costs, even the loss of an escort vessel like ours.

While the fleet was anchored in Lingayan Gulf, three Japanese torpedo bombers we called "Bettys" came in on a run heading for the *Pennsylvania*. They were obviously kamikazes who wanted to drop their torpedoes and then crash their planes into the *Pennsylvania.* Two were shot down quickly, and the third turned tail and fled. The entire force then secured from General Quarters, except for the *Chaffee.*

Commander Jones, our captain, was a cautious man and felt certain the "Betty" would return soon, since he was bent on suicide anyway. He had us stay at our battle stations and did not secure from General Quarters. He could not have been more right, because about ten minutes later the third "Betty" came back, and we could see her silhouetted in the moon. The captain swung the fast little ship around and headed right toward the "Betty," and, without our running lights, we were invisible in the black of night. The startled pilot was forced to change his angle and dropped the torpedo right in front of us, before it had a chance to arm the warhead. The fish landed so close to us that the spray, when it hit the water, wet the officers and men on the bridge. It then hit us in the bow, right at the boatswain's locker, but below the water line, going clean through the bow and out the

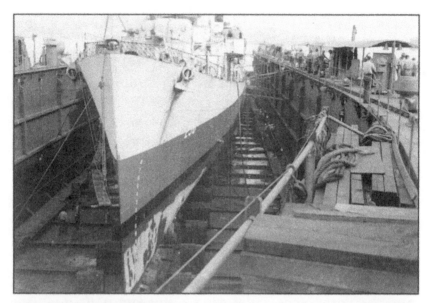

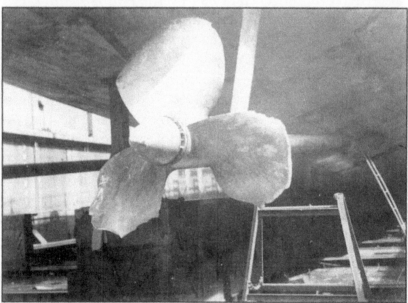

USS Chaffee, Destroyer Escort, in dry dock undergoing repairs for damage suffered by the kamikaze "Betty" bomber who dropped a torpedo which went through the boatswain's locker at the bow and out the other side but never exploded. Note damage to propeller when the ship hit a coral reef during the Battle of Lingayan Gulf, Luzon, the Philippine Islands.

other side. The forward compartment immediately filled with seawater, and although we quickly closed the watertight door, we began to list. But other than that we were all safe and unhurt. The ship was difficult to control, and we hit a coral reef with our propellers, causing the props to become damaged and require replacement. In the meantime, the kamikaze was shot down.

The following morning, the flotilla commander came aboard to congratulate us on saving the *Pennsylvania,* and they in turn sent over some spare parts we needed, as well as lots of ice cream and other goodies we could not make on our ship. Finally, we were towed to an LSD (Landing Ship Dock) where the water could be pumped out and the ship repaired. During repairs, C.D. Smith found one of the propellers from the torpedo and mounted it on a plaque for all to see. The entire story of the *Chaffee* has been written in a book by Lt. Lewis M. Andrews, called *Tempest, Fire, and Foe.* It is the story of all the Destroyer Escorts that turned the tide of the naval war and destroyed many enemy submarines, making submarine warfare ineffective for

The Majestic USS Chaffee (DE-230)

the rest of the war. It is interesting to note that the records of the Nazi sub fleet show that the cost in men and boats were no longer worth the effort once the mighty Destroyer Escorts came onto the scene. Lt. Andrews covered every Destroyer Escort ever built and explained that since all six-hundred had already been scrapped, and the crews that manned them were dying off so fast, he was afraid that the story of the DE's and the way they changed the naval war would be lost forever. So he spent eight years compiling all the information together to write the book and preserve the DE story forever. The chapter on the *Chaffee* is entitled, "Rendezvous With a Friendly Torpedo."

It was shortly after that incident that word came down that the Navy was forming a new amphibious force and needed men to man those new ships. They said that anyone who volunteered would get a thirty-day leave and then would report to the amphibious training school at Little Creek, Virginia. No one had ever seen these new ships; the scuttlebutt was that it was a suicide squadron, and so on. Well, no one in our electrical gang volunteered, so we had to draw straws. The fellow who got the short straw was devastated because he was older than most of us and had a wife and two children and did not want to go to the suicide squadron. That same day, we got our mail from home, and I received a "Dear John" letter from my girl whom I had not seen in almost two years. She was dating a 4F, and I wanted to go home to see what it was all about. I spoke with the sailor who drew the short straw and we switched, and I went home for my thirty-day leave. I decided then that she was not worth it and, after a nice leave, I left to report to Little Creek and the "amphibs."

Electrician's Mate C.D. Smith holds the propeller of the torpedo which fell off into the boatswain's locker as it went through and out the other side.

Chapter Five

The New Amphibious Forces Dubbed the Suicide Squad or The Expendables

I t was strange to take training to man a ship none of us had ever seen, not even a picture of one, as it was all hush-hush for security reasons. Our training was unusual in that General Quarters (battle stations) were in weird places. On the *USS Chaffee,* my battle station as an engineer was in the engine room, but on the LSM, it was, of all places, topside and at the bow of the ship. I later learned that I was to open the bow doors and lower the ramp so the soldiers and the jeeps and tanks could get off. We also learned, for the first time, the reason for the fleet of LSMs being built. Heretofore, the soldiers would come on large troop transports or LSTs then hit the beach on LCIs (Landing Craft Infantry). As everyone knows, the LCI would be helpless on the beach after the soldiers disembarked, and the operator of the LCI, a Boatswain or Cox'n mate, was usually killed. The new amphibs, however, were totally different. They were much larger than an LCI-203 feet, with a stern anchor winch. They would drop the stern anchor (a Danforth anchor) in deep water, then hit the beach. After all the men and machines were ashore they would close bow doors and reverse the anchor winch and pull the ship off the beach and put her back in action. She had light armament consisting of 50 cal. machine guns, 20mm and 40mm anti-aircraft guns, and depth charges as well. Who knows, one of those odd little ships with a flat bottom may have even sunk a Japanese submarine. We called the ship a "floating bathtub," but those sturdy little ships took us all the way to Japan and distinguished themselves in battle. They and their seasick crews will never be forgotten, because there is one of them, LSM-45, moored at Freedom Park in Omaha, Nebraska, for the entire world to see. It was interesting to learn that the many LSMs were scrapped, but the 45 was given to the Greek navy and was recently returned at the request of the LSM/LSMR Association and moved at great cost to Freedom Park, where it has been restored exactly as it was when it served the U.S. Navy. Most of the work was donated by veterans who served on those ships, and it was arranged through the LSM/LSMR Association. The money needed was raised by private contributions, mostly from veterans who served aboard those ships.

Upon completion of our training, I received an award for being first in the class and was promoted to electrician's mate second class (EM2/c). I was then sent back to the Brooklyn Navy Yard to attend the

Honolulu, Hawaii, on one of the LSM 472 stops, 1945.

The Navy Hymn

Eternal Father, strong to save,
Whose arm doth bind the restless wave,
Who bidd'st the mighty ocean deep,
Its own appointed limits keep;
O hear us when we cry to thee
For those in peril on the sea.

O Savior, whose almighty word
The wind and waves submissive heard,
Who walked'st on the foaming deep,
And calm amidst its rage did sleep;
O hear us when we cry to thee
For those in peril on the sea.

O Sacred Spirit, who didst brood
Upon the chaos dark and rude,
Who bad'st its angry tumult cease,
And gavest light and life and peace;
O hear us when we cry to Thee
For those in peril on the sea.

O Trinity of love and power,
Our brethren shield in danger's hour;
From reck and tempest, fire and foe,
Protect them whereso'er they go,
Thus ever let there rise to thee
Glad hymns of praise from land and sea.

Commissioning Ceremonies
USS LSM-472
23 March 1945

Sperry Gyrocompass School, since I would be in charge of the maintenance of the compass, which is an important piece of equipment necessary to keep the ship on course. It is interesting to note that the Gyrocompass must be cleaned regularly and only with 100 proof alcohol, so that there is no residue that can set the compass off course. I remember that when we were at Saipan Island, after the battle, I ran out of alcohol and sent one of my men, Fireman 1st Class Rudy Von Ruden, ashore with a requisition for a gallon of alcohol. Rudy was a regular navy man who had been in the service since before the war. He had one very bad habit — he drank. Many times he was AWOL. He was a good electrician and my right hand man, though, and I learned a lot about naval ship electricity from him. He went ashore for our supplies, and later, when I went to use the alcohol, it turned out to be a five-gallon can. I questioned him about it, and he explained that it was all they had. Some time later I went to use it again, and it was just about all gone. That much alcohol would clean the compass of several ships for the duration of the war, so I knew something was wrong. I questioned Rudy and the rest of the electrical gang without success. One night, Rudy was to relieve me on watch in the engine room, but he never showed up. I went to get him, and he was dead drunk. I could not believe it, but apparently he had made some of his "Kickapoo Joy Juice," as he called it, by putting some alcohol in a can, putting a piece of gauze bandage over the top, and then putting some yeast on top of that and letting it ferment. It was his own private still, and he stored the rest of his "juice" in the water kegs on the life rafts of the ship after spilling out the drinking water. If we had to use the rafts, we would have been the drunkest sailors in the fleet. That night, when I finally woke him, he started to scream that he was blind, and, in fact, he was temporarily, as the pharmacist mate, Doc Morrell, explained to me. He would certainly have been court marshaled, so we put water back in the kegs and we took turns at his watch until he was back on his feet. Needless to say, we never saw any "Kickapoo Joy Juice" ever again!

Back at the Sperry Gyrocompass School, we received our orders to leave for the LSM-472, which had just been completed in Houston, Texas. We arrived, and I finally saw her for the first time. We immediately named her the "Giant Bathtub." It was strange and a little frightening to see a crew of fifty-four boys, mostly eighteen to twenty years of age, and the same for the officers. Captain Barnes was about twenty-five; the Executive Officer, Lt. JG Richard M. Cyert was twenty-three; and I was twenty. Most of us had never been to sea, except for myself and a couple of others. So it was a green ship, of a type never seen before, and a crew of kids still wet behind the ears that set sail from Houston, through the Panama Canal, and into the Pacific.

When the 472 arrived in Acapulco, after an uneventful trip through the Panama Canal, we had been aboard for some time since leaving Houston, and no one had been given any liberty. This was a foreign country, and a swinging one at that, and the entire crew was ready to go ashore. Captain Barnes asked our executive officer, Lt. Cyert, to pick someone to act as a shore patrol, because knowing Acapulco, he was sure the crew would get into trouble. Lt. Cyert suggested myself as the sole SP because he said that I was not only dependable, but that I would never get into trouble in the red light district because I believed all those signs aboard the ship warning about venereal disease. So, off I went, all decked out in my dress blues, leggings, a

"The Pennsy Kid"

Scotty Again

Making Pan-American Relations

The Wolves, at it again

forty-five automatic pistol, and my SP band on my arm. I was told by the lieutenant to keep order in the brothels and to make a list of all the crew who had sexual relations so that upon their return they would be ordered to see the pharmacist mate, Doc Morrell, and apply the necessary medicine to avoid infection.

I squared away my hat as was required for shore patrol duty and left the ship. As I saluted the officer of the deck, Ensign Ed Breznak from New Jersey, he saluted back and said, "I hope you can handle this assignment without joining the party."

Acapulco was really beautiful. Lush, green, and warm. I headed straight for the red light district, and when I arrived, I could see that a lot of the crew was already three sheets to the wind from the tequila they had been drinking. The hot weather wasn't helping either. I said hello to each member of the crew, and when I was certain they had been involved with one of the ladies of the evenings, I jotted down their names in my little black book as ordered. The red light district was about two city blocks long with one-story row houses, each with a front door. In front of each door sat a lady of the evening hawking her wares, usually at two hundred pesos, which is approximately six U.S. dollars.

After some time, when I thought I really had it under control, one of the girls named Lolita came running up to me, leaving her door unattended, and in broken English and mostly Spanish, she shouted she would service me for only 100 pesos. When I refused, she lowered the price even more to 50 pesos, and then in desperation, hanging onto my arm all the while, she shouted for "amour, no pesos." I was stunned this time and could see all my crew members laughing at this ridiculous scene. When I refused once again, she replied, "Let me see it!" I responded, "See what?" "You know," she said, "the biggest one in the U.S. Navy!" I finally got away from her as she tried to grab the family jewels!

When I returned to the ship after the last crewman was aboard and accounted for, Lt. Cyert and Captain Barnes asked how it went and if I had any trouble. I told them that the only unusual incident was when Lolita tried to grab me and I didn't know why. At this point, everyone started to laugh, because the word was out about what happened. It seems that Lolita had asked one of the crew why I had a gun, leggings, and a SP band. His answer was that I was the most endowed sailor in the U.S. Navy and that I had to wear the leggings so it would not fall onto the floor and drag along as I walked. The .45 automatic was to protect me from girls like her, and the SP band stood for "Super Penis." You can just imagine my embarrassment at not only being the butt of a joke, but that everyone, including Lt. Cyert and Captain Barnes, knew about the set-up except for me. I did, however, get even. No one would

Wilbur Helmerich and Zoot Sims with a Mexican policeman at Acapulco, Mexico. (Will became a doctor after the war.)

The famous Sardis Restaurant in Los Angeles, CA. Left to right: Timmons, Ed Rhodes, Chuck Patterson and the author.

tell me who told Lolita, so I put all the crew's names in my report, and they all had to see Doc Morrell. So I had the last laugh after all.

Life aboard the 472 was good in those days, far from the war on a brand new ship, with lots of new friends. Lt. Cyert was a very serious but nice fellow, who, at age twenty-three, had been a teacher at Minneapolis University. He interviewed each of the crew one at a time so that he could fit them into their proper station aboard ship where they could do their best for the ship and the other crewmembers. One morning, he called for me over the intercom and I reported to the officer's mess where he held these interviews. He asked me why I had no high school diploma, since my grades at Purdue and Sperry were very good, and I replied that I never did graduate high school, having left in the middle of the semester to join the Navy. He then said he was promoting me to electrician's mate first class (EM1/c) and was putting me in charge of the ship's electrical gang. He also told me that if I would agree to take some correspondence courses from his college, he would act as my teacher, but only if I did promise to complete my high school education and go on to college (if we survived the war). He also made a note in my records that, if possible, I should be assigned to Officer's Candidate School. We became the best of friends after that interview, and he helped me whenever possible with my studies. We went on liberty together, which was strange for an officer and an enlisted man. He was a very quiet and shy young man, and I would always ask any date that I had to bring a blind date for him. It always seemed to work out just fine, as you can see from the picture of us at the Tropicana nightclub.

One day, after being out at sea for some time, Lt. Cyert told me that the crew seemed to be bored, since we had not yet caught up with Compac 75 to which we were assigned, or homesick, since most of the crew had only been in the service a few months and only a few, like myself, had been to sea before. He asked if I had any ideas to help the morale of the crew. I suggested we try to get a 16mm sound movie projector, which the larger ships had issued to them, and a movie. I could be the movie operator and show a movie whenever we were at anchor and trade movies with the larger ships that had movies. In addition, I asked if we could get some of those V-discs I had read about in the *Stars and Stripes* and a turntable so I could play the music while at anchor over the intercom. We were not allowed to listen to radio while underway because we might be located by the enemy, and, besides, we hated to turn on the radio even in port because we constantly were bombarded by Tokyo Rose, an American turncoat, I believe, of Japanese background. She had a soft, almost pleading kind of voice, and she would tell all our personnel that fighting was useless, and that the Imperial Japanese navy had destroyed the U.S. Navy, and that we should surrender to save ourselves and all our shipmates from destruction. She would go on and on about our own family and sweethearts back home whom we would never see again if we did not surrender.

Lt. Cyert was impressed and thanked me for all of my suggestions. At our next stop at Pearl Harbor, he requisitioned the equipment we needed and put me in charge as the official movie operator and disc jockey. Whenever possible, I would announce over the intercom by first blowing my boatswain's pipe, which I still own to this very day. "Now here this," I would say. "Tonight's movie will be *Andy Hardy's Double Trouble*, starring Mickey Rooney, at 1900 hours on the fantail." When it was possible to play the V-discs, provided I was not on watch or otherwise at other duties, I would announce via the intercom, again with my boatswain's pipe, "Now hear this! We will be playing V-discs for the next hour or so, and any requests to this disc jockey will be welcome and honored." I would then announce who requested it, such as, "Here's a request from EM2/c Josh Cope for *GI Jive*, by Johnny Mercer and the Andrew Sisters." The crew and officers loved it, and for a while I was a hero — until we weren't able to trade movies and they were fed up with Andy Hardy. I then came up with an idea for a ship's newspaper to be published twice a month. I called it the *Tank Deck Star*, and we did it on the radioman's typewriter and then ran off copies on our mimeograph machine. When I see the new technology of today, I realize we were living in the dark ages in the 1940s, but to us it was what we thought was the best technology available, and at the time, it was.

I am reprinting the first issue of the *Tank Deck Star,* of which I was the editor-in-chief. My best pal, EM2/c Josh Cope, was my associate editor, and believe it or not he had the original copy, which he gave me fifty-four years later when we both ended up in Pennsylvania. Josh is now gone, but I will never forget him. He was the oldest member of the crew, even older than the captain was at age twenty-six, with a lovely wife, Elizabeth, back in Landsdale, Pennsylvania, and a son as well. I am reprinting that issue to indicate what was on the minds and in the hearts of every last one of those young sailors, most of whom were away from home and the USA for the very first time in their short lives.

En route to Texas via Pullman

Rollin Simon Wolf *Bunch of the crew at Little Creek*

EXTRA   *THE*   EXTRA

* * * * * *TANK-DECK STAR* * * * *

ALL THE NEWS THAT
NO OTHER PAPER   WEATHER REPORT
WOULD PRINT   THE FIRST OVER SEAS EDITION   ----   NICE IF IT DOESN'T RAIN
      ***
      (IN FACT THE VERY FIRST EDITION)   APRIL, 1945

STAFF

EDITOR IN CHIEF- AL PINCUS EM2/C
     ***
FEATURE- J. M. COPE F1/C
     ***
ARTICLES- MELVIN C. DUNAVANT F1/C
     ***
REPORTERS- LOUIS M. BENVIGNATI S1/C
          WILLIAM E. TURNER S2/C
          EDWARD W. RHODES S1/C
     ***
ART- RALPH J. DENU F1/C
      EDWARD WILLIAM RHODES S1/C
     ***
QUIZ- RAY TEXEL BM2/C

SPORTS

BY MELVIN C. DUNAVANT

FLASH! FLASH! AND ALL THE SHIPS AT SEA. LETS GO TO PRESS. THIS IS YOUR SPORTS REPORTER WITH HIGHLIGHTS OF THE WEEK. FIRST WE TAKE UP THE SUBJECT OF BOXING, ONE OF AMERICA'S FOREMOST ACTIVITIES. I HAD THE HONOR OF BEING A GUEST AT OUR FIRST OUTDOOR BOXING MATCH OF THE GOOD SHIP LSM 472. IT WAS A LITTLE LATE WHEN I ARRIVED BUT THE BOUTS THAT WERE STAGED ON MY ARRIVAL WERE THE BEST OF THE EVENING. MR. CYERT, OUR VERSATILE EX. OFFICER DONED THE GLOVES WITH ONE OF OUR BETTER KNOWN BEEF TRUSTS AND PROCEEDED TO BRING DOWN THE PRICE OF MEAT. IT WAS A GOOD BOUT AND OUR SEAMAN HILL TRIED TO GET IN HIS SUNDAY PUNCH BUT WAS ALWAY'S A DAY LATE, GOOD CLEAN FUN. THEN THE BOUT OF THE EVENING, KID SPIKE PATTERSON WEARING ONE OF COPE'S

(CONTINUED ON PAGE 3)

HELP MAKE THE JAPPY,
LOOK PRETTY SAPPY,
BUY MORE WAR BONDS, AND SPEED VICTORY

EDITORIAL

BY R.M. CYERT, LT. (JG) EX. OFF.

WELL, OUR PAPER HAS FINALLY BEEN BORN. PINCUS HAD THE IDEA ABOUT TWO DAYS AFTER COMMISSIONING, I BELIEVE. BUT NATURALLY, IN HOUSTON, WHO WAS THINKING OF GETTING OUT A PAPER? AND I UNDERSTAND LONG BEACH, LOS ANGELES, AND HOLLYWOOD WERE ALSO "FAIR" LIBERTY POINTS. BUT NOW THAT WERE TAKING THELONG WAY HOME, WE'LL HAVE PLENTY OF TIME AND THAT'S WHERE THE PAPER COMES IN.

THINGS CAN REALLY BE DULL ABOARD SHIP AS EVERYONE HAS SEEN. AND IT'S UP TO US TO ENTERTAIN OURSELVES. A PAPER LIKE THIS CAN BE A LOT OF FUN. EVERYONE GETS A CHANCE TO KID EVERYONE ELSE, BUT ALL HANDS MUST COOPERATE OR THE IDEA LOSES IT'S PUNCH. SO IF YOU SEE OR HEAR SOMETHING THAT AMUSES YOU, MAKE SURE IT GETS IN THE PAPER SO WE ALL CAN BE AMUSED TO. WE SURE NEED IT.

THE END

TEXEL'S QUIZ COLUMN

1. YOU PUT IT ON THE TABLE, YOU CUT IT. YOU PASS IT AROUND, YET YOU DON'T EAT IT.

2. EVERYTHING IN THE UNIVERSE IS DOING PHYSCIALLY RIGHT NOW REGARDLESS, OR WEATHER IT IS A ANIMAL, VEGETABLE, OR MINERAL AND REGARDLESS OF WHERE IT IS.

3. WHAT IS PART OF YOU THAT FRIENDS USE MORE THAN YOU DO.

(ANS. NEXT WEEK)

PAGE 2

THE TATTLER

SEES NOTHING KNOWS NOTHING TELLS ALL
BY J.M. COPE F 1/C

STRAIGHT FROM JOSH'SCROCK SHOP......

IS THERE A FEUD BREWING BETTWEEN NICK
THE GREEK AND LITTLE JOE THE IRSH....

ASK DIETZ WHAT HE DID WITH THAT BOX..

WILL MR. DIBOLL'S HYDROGEN PLANT PROVE
A SUCCESS OR DOES HE HAVE ANOTHER USE
FOR THOSE (THINGS)?....................

I HOPE WE GET ANOTHER BUNCH OF PASSANGERS
SOON, THESE GUYS ARE GETTING ONTO DOC'S
CANDY. AND SPEAKING OF THE BOOT CARGO IF
THERE WERE 40 MORE TEXEL WOULD STILL
FIND ENOUGH DETAILS FOR ALL OF THEM....

SO WE ALL DON'T APPROVE OF PINKY'S
PROGRAM....WHATS THE MATTER WITH IT
WAVER-(SACK-DUITY)...................

WELCOME TO OUR CREW, RAHL NICKOLSON,
SUCKIEL AND HARRISON, IS THERE A CHAPLAIN
STRIKER AMOUNGST YOU..................

WE'LL SURE BE GLAD WHEN JONE'S GETS OFF
OF THIS 4-8 WATCH, OR WILL HE STILL
GET UP EARLY TO HAUNT THE REST OF US
LATE SLEEPERS................

WE HAVN'T BEEN ABLE TO FIGURE OUT WHY
THE CAPTAINS RIGHT SHOE IS CUT UP--
IS SOMEONE STEPPING ON HIS TOES?....

TO MR. CYERT--- DOES YOUR LEFT CHEEK
FEEL DIFFERENT LATLY ....

CONGRATULATIONS IN ADVANCE TO THOSE
MEN GETTING RATED ON THE 1 ST........

WE ALL WONDER IF LOLA BACK IN
ACAPULCO STILL THINKS OF PINKY AND
CAMP ????????????????...............

THEY'LL NEVER LIVE IT DOWN

BY AL PINCUS EM 2/C

HAVE YOU HEARD ABOUT THE TIME
WHEN JIM GORMAN OUR STOREKEEPER
WENT ASHORE TO GET OUR PAY
ACOUNT.....
WHEN HE RETURNED HE FOUND THE
SHIP HAD LEFT A LITTLE AHEAD
OF SCHEDULE.
A COAST GUARD CUTTER BROUGHT
HIM OUT TO THE SHIP, AND AS THE
BOAT DREW ALONGSIDE , THERE
STOOD GORMAN ON ITS DECK YELLING
"MR. CYERT WHAT SHALL I DO NOW?"
"DID YOU KNOW THAT???????????

I SUPPOSE WE ALL REMEMBER THE
NIGHT WE SPRUNG A LEAK IN OUR
PORT STERN TUBE.
TRUELSON ONE OF OUR GREAT MOTOR
MAC'S DISCOVERED THE LEAK,
WHICH BY THIS TIME HAD ALL BUT
FILLED THE AUX. MACHINERY SPACE.
AS HE UNLOCKED THE DOOR IT FLEW
OPEN, AND POOR TRUELSON WAS
FLOORED BY A TORRENT OF SALT
WATER, WHICH INCIDENTALLY RUINED
ALL OF LESH'S COMIC BOOKS .
WHEN OUR EX-FIRST CLASS MOTOR
MAC BERNASCONI ARRIVED ON THE
SCENE, AND BEHELD THE WATER
SOAKED TRUELSON ....
HIS FIRST WORDS WERE
"WHO GAVE YOU PERMISSION TO
TAKE A SHOWER WHILE ON WATCH ?"

IT'S A TOUGH LIFE FELLOWS
ISN'T IT??????????????

FLASH **************FLASH
DID YOU KNOW THAT OUR ESTEEMED
EXEC. LT. CYERT WAS A GUEST AT
THE CAL. STATE SENATE DURNING
OUR STAY IN THAT NOBLE STATE.
HE WAS GIVEN THE PRIVILAGES OF
THE FLOOR, AND BOWED NOBELY TO
ALL CORNERS OF THE FLOOR. HE
THEN SAT DOWN AND REMAINED THERE
FOR ONE HOUR.
IT LOOKS AS THOUGH WE CAN
EXPECT GREAT THINGS FROM HIM....

PAGE 3

SPORTS (CONT. FROM PAGE 1)

SPECIALS WHICH IS A VERSION OF HOW YOU LOOK DOING TWENTY TEARS AT LEAVENWORTH, CAME OUT WITH HONORS IN THE SPORT THAT WAS IN VOUG DURING THE ROMAN DAY'S, THE BOYS WERE CAUTIONED TO WEAR HEAD GEAR TO PREVENT INJURY, BUT BEING TOUGH GATORS AND HAVING FOUGHT THE BATTLE OF LITTLE CREEK, THEY DISDAINED THE THOUGHTS OF SUCH EFIMINITY BOTH BOY'S GAVE A GOOD ACCOUNT OF THEM-SELVES AND A GOOD TIME WAS HAD BY ALL. IF THE PROMOTER CAN FIND A GOOD DEAD BODY WITH NO LIFE, MAYBE I WILL GO A FEW ROUNDS. MAY WE HAVE MANY MORE OF THESE MORALE BOOTERS SOON. YE OLD FIGHT REPORTER

THE END

CLASSIFIED COLUMN
(ADVERTISMENTS)

IS YOUR ELBOW HALF WAY UP YOUR ARM? IS YOUR NOSE IN THE MID-DLE OF YOUR FACE? DO YOU FEEL TIRED BEFORE GOING TO BED AT NIGHT? IF SO, SEE DOC MURRELL, HE'LL FIX YOU ONCE AND FOR ALL.

THE SHIPS MUSIC DEPT. IS ALL OUT OF PHONOGRAPH NEEDLES. WHEN PAY DAY ROLLS AROUND, LET'S ALL CHIP IN TO OUR NEEDLE FUND. LEAVE CONTRIBUTIONS WITH THE RADIO MEN.

LISTEN IN EACH EVENING AT 1800 FOR MUSIC AS YOU LIKE IT. THE PROGRAM THAT PLAYS YOUR FAVOR-ITE PLATTERS WHEN YOU WANT TO HEAR THEM.

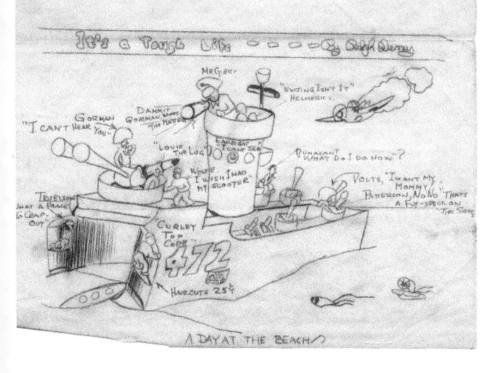

A DAY AT THE BEACH

MEET THE CREW

EACH WEEK WE FEATURE A STORY BASED
ON AN INTERVIEW WITH ONE OF THE
CREW.............................

FOR OUR FIRST ISSUE WE HAVE CHOSEN
OUR COMMANDING OFFICER LT. C.W.
BARNES JR. ....

AS MOST OF US KNOW ALREADY, OUR
COMMANDING OFFICER LT. CHARLES W.
BARNES JR. IS A NATIVE OF JACKSON-
VILLE FLORIDA.
HE ATTENDED BIRMINGHAM-SOUTHER
COLLEGE IN ALABAMA AND WAS A
REPORTER ON THAT INSTITUTIONS
NEWSPAPER. HE WAS ALSO EDITOR OF
THE COLLEGES YEAR BOOK.
MOST OF HIS NAVAL CAREER WAS SPENT
IN THE AMPHIBIOUS FORCES, AND
PRIOR TO BEING ASSIGNED TO THE POST
OF COMMANDING OFFICER OF THE LSM
472, HE WAS ABOARD THREE OTHER
AMPHIBIOUS CRAFT ....
ON THE APA 77 HE WAS BOAT REPAIR
OFFICER AND ON THE APA 26 HE
SERVE AS COMMANDER OF SMALL BOATS
FLOTILLA #1.

HE WAS THEN ASSIGNED TO THE LCI
190 AS ENGINEERING OFFICER. IT
WAS WHILE HE WAS ABOARD THE 190,
THAT HE ENCOUNTERED HIS CLOSEST
CALL DURING ACTION.
AT THE INVASION OF SOUTHERN FRANCE,
HIS SHIP WAS THE FIRST TO HIT THE
BEACH, AND WAS MET BY A WITHERING
POINT BLANK FIRE FROM THE ENEMIES
SHORE BATTIERIES.
SHE TOOK A HIT IN THE TROOPS
QUATERS, BEFORE THE GERMANS WERE
FINALLY DRIVEN AWAY BY 20 M.M.
FIRE FROM THE SHIPS GUNS.
CAPTAINS BARNES REMEMBERS THE
INVASION OF ELBA AS BEING ONE
OF THE TOUGHEST ONES HE WAS IN.
"ALTHOUGH IT WAS A SOMEWHAT SMALL
SCALE INVASION, IT WAS A BLOODY
ONE" HE SAID.
WHEN THE PRESINT CONFLICT SUBSIDES
THE CAPTAIN PLANS TO CONTINUE
HIS WORK IN THE FIELD OF NATURAL
SCIENCE.
INCIDENTLY, TODAY IS THE CAPTAIN'S
BIRTHDAY. CONGRATULATIONS, AND
MANY HAPPY RETURNS OF THE DAY.

DID YOU KNOW THAT WE ARE SLOWER BURNING
AND CONTAIN 28 % LESS NICOTINE --

More atomic logs

Scotty and "Mex Benny"

Scotty pickin' 'em young

"Benny the Bum"

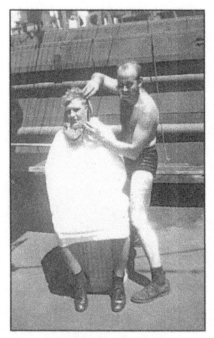

Josh's Crock Shop

20 year man

Fueling at sea

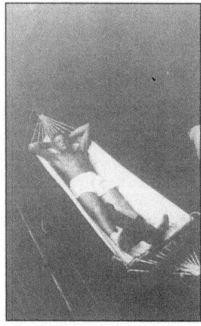

Horizontal Kruz

"Glamour Boy" R.D. Dencker

Chief Boatswain in the making

Natural Position

"Mr. Sexy"

E.H. Rhoades "Horizontal" in center

Chapter Six

Initiation into the Sacred Order of the Golden Dragon and Neptunis Rex, Ruler of the Deep

The U.S. Navy, like most navies the world over, lives by tradition and cherishes those traditions as part of Navy life. In June of 1945, the LSM was bound for the Island of Guam in the Marianas group of islands. As we passed the 180th meridian, we were suddenly told that we would be inducted into the Sacred Order of the Golden Dragon, an old Navy tradition when passing the 180th, which is also the International Date Line. I told our executive officer, Lt. Cyert, that I was already a member of the order, having been initiated aboard the *Chaffee*, and indeed I was already a Shellback, the name given to salty sailors who had passed the 180th and were inducted and initiated into the order. Since almost none of the crew except myself, Fireman 1/c Von Ruden, a regular Navy man, Golden, Boatswain 1/c, and one or two others were Shellbacks, we became the ones in charge of the initiation. The Pollywogs, as new sailors were called, were subjected to the usual indignities, which included a severe haircut, running the gauntlet, and other things designed to make them a salty and respected sailor. Finally, they were issued a sort of diploma, a copy of which is included herein, and they were allowed to wear an earring in their left ear as a sign that they were no longer a pollywog, but in fact were salty sailors now called Shellbacks. Even the officers who had not heretofore been initiated were required to join in and become Shellbacks as well. It was wonderful for morale, because now we had an entire crew of Shellbacks and we all felt pretty salty and special.

Sometime later in July of 1945, we passed the Equator on our way south. We were on course to another romantic island called Tulagi. It was another hellhole of an atoll, which we took back from the Japanese at a substantial loss of life. It was quite confusing, because the Navy had its ships hit some islands and skip others. I think the operation was called "island hopping." Whatever the reasons, it drove the Nippons a little crazy, because they never knew where we would strike next.

Well, as you might have expected, we had another hazing in order to become members of the Order of Neptunis Rex, Ruler of the Deep. We were all Shellbacks now, so it was not as bad as the first time, and if I remember correctly, I was either the Ruler of the Deep or one of his right hand men. It is interesting to note that the tradition continues today, but it is voluntary because of the fact that there are women aboard our warships now.

We were out to sea for some time, and, as most sailors know, the dampness can destroy certain food supplies. After some time had passed, the cook informed us that the bread he was baking daily would also have, as an added ingredient, a flower bug. He told us that they did not eat much, and they might give us some needed protein. At first, we did not eat the bread, but after some time, you got pretty hungry. You want the bread, but not the bugs, so we devised a system that we could live with. When we sat down to chow, someone would yell, "Bread inspection!" and all of us would hold our bread up to the overhead lights so we could see the bugs. Then we would pick them out, and when that was done, the same sailor would say, "two," and we would commence with the meal. It was like a drill, and we all got a kick out of it.

When recalling food aboard the 472, I also remembered an incident that only a 20-year-old sailor would become involved in, and which is indelibly imprinted in my mind. We had been to sea for months and ran out of food, except for cases of sardines in olive oil and hard tack (a hard dry biscuit that resists moisture and can stay edible for a great deal of time). Well, you can imagine the effect on the human digestive system when you consume a can of sardines in olive oil three times a day for a couple of weeks. Everyone on the ship had terrible diarrhea, and the head (toilet) was filled shortly after each meal with a long waiting line. In rough weather, it was not too bad because many of the crew would hang over the side and feed the fish! To add to our misery, we also ran out of toilet tissue. Normally, each crew member would be issued a roll of toilet tissue when necessary, but now it was all gone, so we had to resort to the use of old newspapers, a rather primitive operation which required a great deal of squeezing of the paper in order to make it soft enough for use. The jokes about our predicament included the one that stated that if you missed the paper, you could read it on another shipmate's backside. The head was a rather small compartment, which was fitted with a metal trough on one side, similar to one used for feeding or watering horses. But ours was slanted at the bottom so that the forward end was higher in the bottom than the after end, and there was a large scupper (hole) at the lower end. The ships bilge pumps carrying seawater to the upper end accomplished the flushing, and as it cascaded down to the lower end, it took the waste with it. It was a rather simple arrangement, which kept the head clean at all times. Fitted to the top of this contraption were six seats, each consisting of two molded slats across the top of the trough for seating. On one occasion that I referred to above, all the seats were taken except the forward one at the top of the trough, where there was a sign posted stating, "Reserved for venereal patients only."

The Navy was quite concerned about venereal disease, and there were signs all over the ship warning the sailors about it and insisting that if there were a question, they should apply prophylaxis, which was readily available from the pharmacist mate, Doc Morrell. On the day in question, I was particularly sick and could not wait, so I sat down on this reserved seat. I was the first to ever sit on it, and immediately all hands looked at me and the jokes began to fly. As they became more abusive, I had to get even with them. Suddenly, I had a great idea. I rolled up some of my newspaper into a ball and lit it with a Zippo cigarette lighter. It caught fire immediately, and I dropped it into the water that took it out of the scupper quickly — but not before it singed the bottoms of five of my shipmates! Each one jumped up as if struck by lightning, looked around, but saw nothing since the flaming paper was already out the scupper and into the sea. No one saw what I had done because I was in the forward corner, and in front of us was a blank bulkhead. I got even, but as any twenty-year-old from Brooklyn, I just could not stop there and did it twice more. I now had my private seat and a special secret satisfaction! But as all good things do come to an end,

Lt. Junior Grade Richard M. Cyert, executive officer and later captain, USS LSM-472. At age 23, he was executive officer and, at age 24, captain. He later became a professor at Carnegie Mellon University, Pittsburgh, PA, and after that, president of that same institution for 25 years, until his death in 1998.

I was finally caught. I was chased around the ship by shouts of shipmates to "throw Sparks overboard!"

My salvation was that only the engineering officer, Lt. JG "Pipes" DiBoll, and myself had keys to the gyro compass room in the bowels of the ship. I got in and locked the compartment and stayed there a long while until the executive officer, Lt. Cyert, called me on the sound-powered telephone to tell me that the crew had forgiven me and had a good laugh. He had been sure to tell them that I was the only one who could take care of the Gyro Compass, and without me we might never get home. That was the end of a great adventure, and an incident that made us all laugh and forget our problems of food shortage and the war in general, even if for only a short time. It all really only went away when we arrived at Tulagi Island and took on supplies

Jerry Canon, gunner's mate 2/c, and "Pops" Kuykendahl, cox'n, with a 20mm machine gun, somewhere in the South China Sea.

(but NO SARDINES!). The only good thing was that I had a private seat in the head until we decommissioned the ship at Portland, Oregon, after the war.

In the meantime, back aboard the 472, still island hopping, we were able to have bread, with the usual inspection, and some delicacies such as SOS (shit on a shingle), which I thought was not too bad. It consisted of a piece of creamed chipped beef on a piece of toasted bread, a mainstay of the Navy in those days.

We transported many army troops, with their jeeps and Sherman tanks carefully stowed on the tank deck (or well deck, as it was referred to). Temperatures topped 100 degrees many a day, and there was also high humidity. We were able to make fresh water from seawater in our distilling units, but when we had troops aboard we could not get our usual every-other-day fresh-water shower and had to give a day to the troops. When the third day came around, you could not stand yourself (or anyone else, for that matter) and could not wait until it was your turn for a shower. We were quite cruel at times and told the troops they could take salt-water showers whenever they wanted. It was all right while you were wet, but in that heat, when you dried up you were stiff as a board and your hair was like some of today's rock and rollers, sticking up and out in every direction. Needless to say, we could all think of better places to be, but we did our duty and the rest is history.

The electrical gang aboard the 472, from left the author, Josh Cope, Chuck Patterson, Rudy Von Ruden, Jr. Vaughn.

The good ship LSM-472 and the 265 on the beach in the Pacific.

The 472 has unloaded and is ready to pull back to sea. The sailor is the author, checking out the ramp.

Chapter Seven

The Novel Ways to Keep Busy
While the Ship is Anchored

Believe it or not, even in wartime, the sailors can get bored when they are safe and at anchor. This brings to mind what we in the crew called "Barnes Folly." Our captain, Lt. Barnes, was an avid sailor and had the machinist mate, my good friend Warren Robertson, with whom I am still in touch, requisition two spare aircraft fuel tanks made of aluminum and weld together a pontoon boat similar to a catamaran. The carpenter's mate then made a mast and boom, and the sail-maker made a sail for the boat. The captain was very proud of his personal sailboat, and whenever we were at anchor in a calm cove or harbor, he would have the deck hands and the boatswain's mate, Tex Texel from New Jersey, lower his pride and joy, "Barnes Folly," over the side, and he would go for a sail. He usually took one of the other officers with him. His favorite sailing pal was Ensign Ed Bresnak from New Jersey. The sailboat never really worked. It was not properly balanced and would turn over, and we would have to fish it and the officer out of the water. But the captain never gave up, and he even had the machinist's mate requisition an old three-horsepower outboard motor, which the poor guy worked on for weeks to get

Barnes Folly

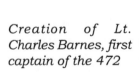

Creation of Lt. Charles Barnes, first captain of the 472

Capt. Barnes seated

The captain's folly

it operational. That didn't work too well either, and finally the captain gave up his hopes for a good sail on "Barnes Folly," and he gave the boat away.

In the meantime, I kept playing the V-Discs over the intercom whenever possible, as well as showing the movie *Andy Hardy's Double Trouble.* It was a good crew, and everyone did their job. Doc Morrell would have sick call every morning, and his favorite medication was tincture of methiolate, which he would put on any wounds with a swab wrapped around a tongue depressor. He was very proud of his favorite medication, and his other favorite was apc tablets (a type of aspirin), and with those tools he kept the crew alive and healthy. One morning, I had a very bad sore throat and got in line at the sick bay. When Doc got to the guy in front of me, he asked the usual question: "What is your complaint?" The guy replied, "I have jock itch, and I got it bad." Doc asked him to drop his pants, and he proceeded to swab the methiolate onto the affected area. Upon finishing up with the guy in front of me, Doc then asked me what my problem was. I quickly replied, "I had a sore throat, but it's gone now!"

One particularly hot and humid day while we were at anchor at one of the smaller islands (I believe it was Tinian), someone suggested to the captain that it would be nice if the crew could take a swim. The captain approved it and ordered me to open the bow doors and lower the ramp so they could dive off it and get back aboard by way of Jacob's ladder hanging from the ramp. It was a great idea — but what about the possibility of sharks? Accordingly, Lt. JG Tex Caldwell, our gunnery I officer, volunteered to stand guard with a 50-caliber machine gun. He did, and, fortunately, he never had to use it. I really think that disappointed him.

Motor Machinist Mate Warren Robertson

Leonard Kearney, Signalman (Flags)

Electrician's mates unloading a bulldozer on Okinawa. From left: Josh Cope, Chuck Patterson, Jr. Vaughn, the author.

We also had a ship's store, which not every LSM had, where you could buy everything from toothpaste to cigarettes. We were the envy of Compac 75, because we had a ship's store, a movie projector, and a disc jockey with about sixty-five hits of the day on V-Discs. We really were special. I bought cigarettes whenever the store was open, even though I have never smoked. They were only a dollar a carton, if you can believe that! They were 20 Grand, Wings, and the rest of the cheapies of the day, and I hoarded them because I knew that I might need them someday to trade with. That day came more than once before the war was over.

One night, while anchored with an armada of ships at Okinawa, I heard the familiar boatswain's pipe, and the boatswain said over the intercom, "Now hear this, Sparky! Lay down the wardroom and report to the captain on the double." I hurried down to the Officers Quarters and found the captain in the wardroom. He said, "Sparks, you have got to get us a new movie, or we will have a mutiny. The crew just can't take *Andy Hardy's Double Trouble* anymore. They know it by heart, and they are beginning to act it out, so take the dinghy and the outboard motor and the machinist mate, as well as a signalman, and try to trade with someone." I said that I would, and I blew my boatswain's whistle and said, "Now hear this, signalman Kearney and machinist's mate (I do not remember his name, but he was a short heavy sailor from Kentucky, built like a bear), lay down to the fantail on the double." By the time I picked up the movie and got to the fantail, they were already there! I explained to them what we had to do. Kearney was as thin as I was, and if we stood sideways, you almost could not see us, but the machinist's mate looked like a line-

Gunnery Officer LTjg Tex Caldwell

The officers of the 472 from left: Rear Ensign Abrams, Ensign Ed Breznak, LTjg Wally Pipes Diball. Front Row: Lt. R.M. Cyert.

backer from any angle. I asked him if the outboard motor was working, and he replied that it was. After all, he had worked on it for days, and it was ready to go. I then called to Boatswain Texel and asked him to lower the boat so we could be on our way. There was a slight chop in the bay, so I lashed the film case to one of the seats and we were off. The machinists started the engine, and, much to our surprise, it sputtered and then caught on. Kearney had his signal flags with him and asked me what to do. I told him to signal every ship we came close to and ask if they wanted to trade with us and that we had an Andy Hardy movie. Every ship had already seen it, and it must have been the one the Navy had most of. That probably was why we got it in the first place!

Now, dear reader, you probably know that in those waters, it can be sunny one moment and you can have a typhoon the next minute. Well, that is exactly what happened to us. One moment the sun shown brightly and the next moment it got dark, windy, and rainy like you seldom see in the Western Hemisphere. We bobbed around like a cork, and I ordered the machinist to turn about and head back to our ship on the double! The rain was unbelievable, as was the wind, and as we came about, the engine faltered and died. Now we were really bobbing around, while Mr. Kentucky, the smart guy who had assured us the engine was in great shape, was frantically tugging on the starter rope. Finally, the big bear gave such a tug that the engine came right off the stern, and, since it was so wet, it slipped out of his hands and went straight to Davey Jones locker, along with Andy Hardy and his girlfriends, never to be seen again.

By this time, the wind had pushed us out toward the sea. We had no oars or bailing can and were now knee-deep in water. We saw one last LST between us and the raging open sea. Kearney frantically tried to wave his signal flags to get their attention, but the flags were also wet, and he was not doing well. The ship's signalman knew we were in trouble, and he signaled Kearney with his blinker light, telling us it was too rough to lower a boat, but they would lower a Jacob's ladder over the side and we should swim for it. I yelled to abandon ship, and then Kentucky informed us that he could not swim! "What the hell are you doing in the Navy if you can't swim?" demanded Kearney. No reply. I yelled that if we passed the LST, the next stop was Japan, and I was not ready for that. We then all jumped off the sinking boat into the rough waters. Kearney grabbed one of Kentucky's arms, and I grabbed the other and yelled to him to kick his feet, which he did, and he, fortunately, learned how to swim at that very moment! The wind helped push us alongside the LST. The Jacob's ladder was already in place, and we grabbed it. As we pulled Kentucky over to the ladder, he grew frantic and climbed right over us, stepping on my knuckles along the way. We came aboard and explained why we were in the dinghy in the first place. The signalman then tried to send a message to our ship that we were safe, but to no avail. They could not use the radio since we were in a war zone, and the orders were for radio silence. They gave us dry clothes and a meal, as well as a place to sleep in the soldiers' bunks, since they were long gone and fighting for Okinawa Island. The Japanese were in caves and in an intricate system of underground tunnels, and it was a terrible battle that caused us to lose about 5,400 men. Thank God that President Truman was a man of no nonsense convictions and dropped the atom bomb on Hiroshima. While I feel sorry for those civilians, I can assure you that had he not taken that difficult step, the war would have continued for another two or more years, with untold loss of life on both sides.

We all knew that once Okinawa was secure, we would be on our way to the mainland of Japan. As it happened, we were, but as the victors instead of an invading force. I still remember working on some equipment on the Tank Deck when we were told over the intercom that President Roosevelt had died. We were stunned. We did not know much about Harry Truman, except that he had been a haberdasher, not the kind of man you would think could rise to the occasion. But rise he did, and he became one of the strongest presidents we ever had, a little George Washington in a modern fedora.

The next morning, the sun shown brightly, and you could almost not imagine that the horror of the night before had ever taken place. The boatswain of the LST lowered a boat and took us back to the 472. We thanked him and came aboard to cheers from our crew, who had been convinced that we had perished in the typhoon. Immediately over the intercom we heard, "Now hear this, Sparks! Lay down to the wardroom on the double." I hurried down, thinking that Captain Barnes was going to tell me he was glad that I had not drowned and maybe even congratulate Kearney and me for saving Kentucky. My elation was short-lived when I saw his face. "Where is the movie?" he bellowed. I could not help but feel that he was being ungrateful and unfeeling. I told him that the film was in Davey Jones' locker, along with the boat and the motor. His reply was that it was my responsibility and that I had better find a way to get a movie before there was a mutiny. I asked if I could go ashore, and he agreed. I felt that the time to use the cigarettes was finally at hand.

The 472 is beached at Wakanoura Wan, a Japanese seaplane base. Everyone is ashore, including Flags Kearney and the author.

I took six cartons and a nice clean set of whites (summer uniform) with me. As we hit the beach, I did not know what I would do on this God forsaken atoll, but I had to try. Then I saw the electrical shack and headed straight for it. I walked in and was stunned to see my old buddy from the *USS Chaffee,* Sal Amico. He jumped over the counter and hugged me, yelling he could not believe it. He was sure he would never see me again after he was given shore duty because he had such chronic seasickness.

I was totally floored by this wonderful reunion in such a God forsaken place. I told him my problem, and he asked what I had to trade. I showed him the six cartons of cigarettes and the uniform. He took them and told me to mind the store and that he would be right back. In about fifteen minutes, he returned with a film case. I could not believe it. I asked him how he did it, because the films were as scarce as hen's teeth. His reply was that I was not to ask questions or tell where I got the film. He apparently had friends on this bloody island. I asked him what movie it was, and he told me that he did not know, but beggars can't be choosers. We said a solemn goodbye and promised to look each other up after the war. But we said it with tongue in cheek, since we knew what would lie ahead for us in the battle of Japan.

I returned to the ship like the conquering hero and was greeted with many congratulatory comments, and even Captain Barnes had a good word. He said he never doubted that I would pull it off; after all, I was from Brooklyn, a place where anything could get done. That night, I walked triumphantly to my movie projector and started the movie, to the delight of the crew. Suddenly, that delight turned to jeers as we saw the name of the movie splashed across the screen. Yes, you guessed it — *Andy Hardy's Double Trouble.* I thought this was really the end for me, but then everyone, including Captain Barnes, started to laugh. The next day, I traded with another ship for *The Maltese Falcon,* staring Humphrey Bogart and Sidney Greenstreet, and, once again, I was the crew's movie hero! The following day, we were allowed to leave the ship and go ashore to hunt for some souvenirs. As we walked along, picking up memorabilia from the battle, I fell into what had been a pillbox at the edge of the beach and landed in the midst of some Japanese soldiers that had committed hari-kari. It was frightening, and the smell of death was sickening. I yelled to my companions, who had to make a human rope to reach me and pull me out. That was the last time I went ashore in Okinawa. From that moment on, I stayed aboard until we got word that the war had ended because of the atomic bomb. We were, of course, elated and wondered what would happen next. We did not have long to wait.

Some of the crew on V-J Day.

Chapter Eight

V-J Day and the
Battleship *Missouri*

Yes, the war was indeed over, and we aboard the 472 were elated, as was everyone else. No more beachheads, bloodshed, and wondering if we would survive. We all thought of home and our loved ones, as well as those who were never going home. All these emotions churned in our heads and hearts as we steamed into the bay along with the rest of the huge armada of ships. It was easily the largest naval force to ever be in one place at one time, and we were privileged to be there and be part of this magnificent and formidable force. I could not help but think about our Navy back on that "Day of Infamy" that was practically destroyed at Pearl Harbor. The *Arizona* and her crew were destroyed quickly, as well as so many more of our ships. I was proud, as I am sure the entire crew of the 472 and indeed the crews of all of those magnificent ships in this armada were, of how we came back from the brink of disaster to become the victors and to turn out to be the largest and most magnificent naval fighting force that the world had ever seen. It warmed my heart to think that it was American "know-how," determination, and ingenuity that made all this possible. "Rosie the Riveter," all the stars in the windows of family homes with men and women in the service, a unified America as never before seen, who together as one, with one voice and one spirit, accomplished the seemingly impossible and brought Nippon to its knees, not to mention the victory in Europe and elsewhere around the globe. It was truly a wonderful day which not one of us will ever forget. It remains always clear in this sailor's memory.

We took our position and dropped our anchor far from the *Missouri* and strained to get a glimpse of the proceedings that memorable day. We had, I thought, not only won the war, but we had made the world and democracy safe for our future generations.

Not long after the surrender was complete, the 472 received orders to beach the ship at a little atoll just off the coast of Wakanoura. It was a seaplane base for the Japanese navy, and we were to take over. Captain Barnes had been transferred before that great day, and Lt. Cyert became our captain. He was a regular guy, and we were all happy to have him as our skipper. He even took liberty with us on occasion, and since he was quite shy, it was my job to see that we got a date for him as well. I sure did arrange a lot of blind dates for him, and we had good times together. On that occasion, as we neared Wakanoura Wan, the boatswain worked his pipe once more. "Now hear this," he said. "All hands will dress in blue uniform so we look like the victors we are." That was obviously from our new captain. He was a proper Ivy League guy and pretty cool at the same time.

We hit the seaplane ramp with the usual thud after dropping our stern anchor and sounding general quarters. My G.Q. station was, as usual, at the bow doors and ramp. I had the sound-powered headphones on, and, as we came to rest, I heard my favorite captain's

The electrical gang of the USS LSM-472 at Okinawa, Japan. Top from left, Cope the Quaker, Sparky, Jr. Vaughan, Chuck Patterson, Rudy Von Rude.

Chuck, Rudy, Sparky, Cope, and in front of the Japanese Flag, Jr. at Okinawa.

voice say, "Sparks, are you ready?" "Aye, aye, sir," I replied. "Open bow doors," sounded the captain. Once again, I replied, "Aye, aye, sir." As I pressed the appropriate Cutler Hammer Switches and the bow doors opened, as always came Captain Cyert's command, "Sparks, lower the ramp." As I pressed the remaining switches and the ramp creaked down, as was my usual duty and as I was taught at Amphib's School, I bent over to be sure that there were no stones or other obstructions under the ramp, so that no one would trip and fall and no jeep would get hung up on the ramp or damaged in any way, not to mention possible damage to my ramp. As I looked at the ramp and the shoreline, I suddenly heard the captain again, but this time his voice was a little anxious. "Sparks, when you stand up, do so slowly and be careful, because there is a Japanese Commander standing right in front of you with a Samurai Sword in his hand and about forty soldiers with rifles behind him." I froze for a moment. Then, as any twenty-one-year-old wise guy from Brooklyn would say, I replied, "Captain, do you think they know the war is over?" The captain said that he had no idea, but that I had better be careful. I came up slow and easy and there in front of me stood a Japanese Commander in his "Sunday best," complete with a very formidable looking Samurai sword raised in his right hand. He looked at me and I at him, neither of us, I believe, knowing what to say or do. Captain Cyert shouted, "Hold your fire men! We don't want to start World War III!" At that moment, the Japanese Commander bowed gracefully, as he said, "Ko-an-itch-i-wa," which means, "Good day to you, sir." He then held out the sword in both hands, horizontally, towards me. I was stunned, and perhaps a little shaken, by the whole incident. I suppose my mouth was hanging open, and I wasn't saying a word. Then I heard my captain once again, saying, "Sparks, take the sword. I think he is trying to surrender to you." I reached out and took the sword, and we both bowed to one another. At that moment, as I accepted the sword, his men dropped their rifles, and, for the old 472, the war was really over. I guess they had gotten word of the surrender. We were indeed in charge, and I had the honor of being first ashore. Signalman Joe Kearney was next, and he took a picture of me as well. The picture, the sword, and a rifle are still in my possession after these past 55 years and hang in my private WWII museum, housed in my converted barn, where they have been for all these years. The captain allowed each of us to take a rifle, and, as I recall, he said the sword was mine since it was surrendered to me. I re-

The US Navy comes ashore at Wakanoura, Japan, immediately after the surrender aboard the USS Missouri. It was indeed a strange feeling as we walked down the streets, which were lined with Japanese civilians. No one said anything, but all had sidearms ready. There was not one unpleasant shout or incident. I believe even the civilians were relieved that it was at last over, especially in view of the atomic bombs dropped on Hiroshima and Nagasaki earlier.

cently had it appraised, and it turns out to be a valuable ceremonial sword which is approximately two-hundred-and-twenty years old. It is forged of only one piece of metal and is very sharp. It has the family name and notches on the end under the handle. It is also perfectly balanced. As for the rifles, they were not state of the art (even for fifty-five years ago), but mine still has the Emperor's seal on it, which they had not enough time to remove, and so that, I am told, makes it very valuable.

I had our sail-maker fashion a cover for each of the items so that I could carry them home without any problem, and they have been a constant reminder to me for over half a century of the war to save democracy and our American way of life. I am extremely proud to have been a part of it and of history as well. The sword and rifle have appeared many times at show-and-tell at school for my children and my children's children, as well as at many lectures I have given on WWII at various libraries and veterans' gatherings. They are truly a part of my life and history, and I prize them highly.

It was shortly after that incident that we were to go ashore in the city of Wakanoura. After that, we landed in Nagoya and so on to many places in Japan, where we spent quite some time before being ordered back to the USA. I was particularly impressed by the orderly takeover of Japan. As soldiers, they were fierce and dedicated fighters, but with the war's end, the Japanese people as a whole were very polite, almost friendly, and I suspect perhaps relieved at knowing the war was over and their home island would not be attacked. In going ashore, as the reader can see in the pictures herein, we were a bit nervous, but all went smoothly, and there were no unpleasant incidents at all.

We settled down for a while as the occupiers, during which time I was able to buy many souvenirs for the family back home. I still had many cartons of cigarettes left in my locker, and these were better than money. Even American candy bars from the ship's store brought excellent prices, and I purchased some beautiful miniature statues of a samurai warrior, a geisha maiden, a Hari Kari Catana (suicide sword), and, best of all, the most beautiful kimono I ever saw, which was for my mom. It was covered with colored artificial gems, and on the back was a large dragon woven into it with gold thread. My mom was impressed, and she kept it for many years. I still have the other items, except for the Geisha girl, which was confiscated by one of my daughters.

As the days passed and we thought of home, we got used to some of the excellent Japanese food, except for sushi, which I still cannot eat. I also have a vivid memory of tangerine trees lining the streets in the countryside and picking them off the tree as we passed by. Our in-house barber, my pal, electrician's mate 2/c Joshua Cope from Pennsylvania, would give haircuts for 25 cents. He was the oldest of the crew at 27 and had a wife and son back home. He had a great sense of humor and loved jazz music as I did, and we got along just fine. When the ship was decommissioned in Portland, Oregon, we said a tearful goodbye. Strange it was that I never forgot any of my shipmates, but especially the old Quaker from Pennsylvania, Josh Cope.

In the year 2000, I found Josh quite by accident. I had joined the LSM/LSMR Vets association and saw a note in their wonderful newsletter about finding old crewmembers. I wrote to them, and they sent me four names in Pennsylvania. The first was Josh Cope. I could not believe my eyes, and I got his phone number from information and discovered that he lived in Lansdale, about a forty-five-minute drive from my place. I called Josh, and he answered the phone. I said, "Is this electrician's mate 2/c Josh Cope of the LSM 472?" There was silence for a moment, then he said, "Who is this?" I replied, "Sparky Pincus, electrician's mate 1/c, your boss aboard the 472." Some more silence, then, "Is it really you, Sparks?" We then spoke for about an hour and finally agreed to meet halfway for lunch at a nice restaurant, The William Penn Inn. It was a good choice, he said, because the inn was older than both of us! Cope then said to me, "How will we know each other after fifty-four years?" My reply was, "Just look for the two oldest guys carrying frayed photo albums." That is exactly how we found each other. He arrived first and was sitting in his car when I hurried by with my photo album under my arm. He called for me: "Hey, Sparks, over here." Needless to say, it was an emotional meeting, and we marveled at how much we really still did look like those crazy kids aboard the 472 so many years ago. We stopped a woman and her young daughter to ask if she would take a picture of us with Cope's camera, and we told her that we were in the Navy together in WWII. She told us that her late father had been in the Navy in WWII, and, suddenly, we felt just a little old!

We had a wonderful lunch, and when we told the waitress we had not seen each other in fifty-four years, she was stunned and told everyone in the place. Suddenly, we were heroes after so many years. We talked about having a reunion and agreed to try to contact other members of our crew. We went over the roster he had and most were gone to the great navy ship in the sky. Others we could not reach, but we did contact at least eight who were close enough for a reunion. Of all these wild kids, it was exciting to learn that one had become a

The author and J. Morris Cope (Josh) when they met in 1999 at the William Penn Inn, Pennsylvania, for a long overdue lunch after not seeing each other for 54 years. This was also a wonderful day for both of us. Josh is gone, but will never be forgotten. When I get what little hair I have left cut, I always think of my favorite ship's barber, Josh, who gave us all the news about the crew and the war as he cut our hair on the ramp for the grand sum of 25 cents.

doctor, another a CIA agent, myself a lawyer, and, the most important one, our captain, Lt. Richard M. Cyert, a professor with a doctorate and the president of Carnegie Mellon University in Pittsburgh for twenty-five years until his death, just eighteen months before Josh and I reunited. That was particularly devastating news for me, since I had been trying to find the lieutenant to tell him I went back to high school and on to become a lawyer and that I owed it all to him because he counseled me and acted as my teacher while aboard ship. Josh did have a letter he had received from Lt. Cyert, which is reprinted in this book. We did contact his widow, who sent me the program from the celebration of her husband's accomplishments at the university. At her request, I made copies of many photos of the lieutenant aboard ship at age twenty-four, long before she knew him.

Motor Machinist Mate 2/c Warren Robertson and the author in my back yard on the occasion of our reunion after 54 years. It was a wonderful day we spent with Josh going through my private WWII museum, meeting my family and having lunch together and just remembering those scary but exciting days we spent together so many years ago.

Dick Hoch, gunner's mate, and wife, Betty, with his family in Montrose, CO.

Jim and Hellen Bjelland on a visit to the Cooleys.

Paul Stevens, another crew member of the 472, looks over one of his pet projects. He has done much racing, most of it on souped-up lawn mowers.

Bill Cooley and his wife, Maureen, at their daughter's home in Virginia recently. Bill became a CIA agent and lived in some interesting places until his retirement.

Sparky's place on the occasion of his reunion with Cope the barber and Warren Robertson. The building houses his antique cars, workshop, and WWII museum. Outside of guest house and museum.

Memorabilia and neon sign adorn the walls of the museum.

Al "Sparky" Pincus holding some of the V-Discs he was given by Captain Cyert after decommissioning the LSM-472. He still plays them on an antique 78 RPM record player.

Sparky and his pride and joy, a 1948 Jaguar, which he restored about 15 years ago and which has won numerous awards and been featured in books and magazines about old cars.

Letter from Lt. Cyert to Josh Cope, 1978

Carnegie-Mellon University
Office of the President
5000 Forbes Avenue
Pittsburgh, Pennsylvania 15213
(412) 621-2600

July 5, 1978

Dear Morris:

It was extremely nice of you to write me. I appreciate it very much.

It is a mighty long time ago that we sailed LSM-472. It sounds as though things have been going quite well for you, except for the two heart attacks. I was sorry to hear about that. I know that if you watch your diet, stay away from smoking, and exercise a lot you can be as good as new. I hope that you are doing that.

I agree with you that duty in the service could have been a lot worse than it was on LSM-472. We had a pretty good time on that ship - particularly after we got rid of the skipper and came to the United States. I never hear from Pincus, Jones, Gitchell, or Texell. I have heard that Wally Diebold is on the engineering faculty at Washington University in St. Louis, but I have not seen him. I saw the former engineering officer on LSM-471. That was the LSM that had the skipper who was a good friend of our skipper. Remember when we pulled into Acapulco. I believe, in fact, he is the fellow I beat so badly during the boxing matches in Guam. I didn't quite have the heart to remind him of it, however. He is now an expert on nuclear energy.

I have been at Carnegie Mellon since 1948, when I got out of graduate school. I got married in 1946 and have three daughters. The youngest one is 19 and is at Harvard in biochemistry. The oldest one has a Ph.D. and has been teaching psychology at a College. The middle one is married and has just made me a grandfather. She lives in Ann Arbor. Her husband works for the Ford Motor Company.

Please give my regards to Lou Benvignatti when you see him. I was sorry to hear that he also had a couple of heart attacks. It must be something in that eastern Pennsylvania air.

If you ever get this way, please be sure to look me up. In the meantime, best of luck to you.

Cordially,

Richard M. Cyert

A Celebration
of
The Life and Memory of

President Emeritus
Richard M. Cyert
(1921 - 1998)

Carnegie Mellon

We had another meeting a few weeks later with Warren Robertson, motor machinist mate 2/c, at my home. We had a wonderful afternoon and a great lunch at a local tavern. They later met some of my family, and we took photos, also reprinted here. We agreed to meet again in a couple of weeks to make further plans for a reunion, and, in the meantime, we exchanged photos and Josh came up with something I had forgotten all about. He had the original copy of the ship's weekly newspaper, the *Tank Deck Star*, which was my brainchild and of which I was editor. I reprint it here (see pages 55-58) to show the reader what we were doing and what was important to nineteen- and twenty-year-olds in the middle of a world war.

Two weeks later, the day before we were to meet again, I received a call from Josh's son informing me that his father had passed away peacefully in his sleep at age eighty-one. Warren and I were devastated, as were the others with whom we were planning the reunion. Of course, we cancelled the reunion for the time being, since we had lost one of the prime movers in the effort to have a reunion. I was at least thankful, as was Warren, that we had the chance to renew an old friendship. Josh's wife, Elizabeth, told me that in those last weeks of his life he was a very happy man for having found us.

I only wish that I had been able to locate Lt. Cyert as well before his passing and experience the kind of closure with him as I did with Cope, the "laughing Quaker."

Since we lost Cope, Warren and I have kept in touch, and we have met twice since then and have relived some of those exciting times we were a part of. It certainly is strange how each member of the crew seems to remember certain things that other members do not and vice versa, and it is nice then to be able to fill the gaps in your memory and come up with a full and continuous saga.

Chapter Nine

A Peaceful Trip to the USA and Home

After an extended time, as part of the occupation in Japan, we finally received orders to take our ship back to Bremerton, Washington, a suburb of Seattle, where we stayed for a while at the Naval Base at Puget Sound. We then were told that the old 472 would be decommissioned and placed in the mothball fleet at Puget Sound. Many of these ships were used later in the Korean conflict, but ultimately they were all scrapped, as were the Destroyer Escorts I served with as well. I could never quite accept that end for those magnificent ships that had taken us all over the world and brought us home safely. Looking at today's navy, I can see that those old ships would be considered antiques along with their crew. Fortunately, one of them, LSM-45, was recently discovered in Greece. It was given to the Greek Navy by the U.S. government as a gift. It was returned to the LSM/LSMR Association and transported at great cost to Freedom Park in Omaha, Nebraska, where it has been lovingly restored to its original glory as a warship of the U.S. Navy. Much of the work was donated by former sailors who had manned those great warships, and the work still continues. It is a sight to see and was the site of a massive reunion of amphib sailors in 1999, with many of the old crews and a few from the LSM-45, who crawled all over the ship remembering various happenings aboard her and her sister ships. Now it stands at Freedom Park as a monument to the amphibious forces and the men that manned those floating, yet majestic, bathtubs all the way to Japan and back.

One of the old crew of the 45, a quartermaster, found the old charts with his handwriting in the bottom drawer of the chart table, fifty-four years after he had placed them there.

Decommissioning was a big job, and we literally stripped the ship to a certain extent. Then they were anchored in the sound, tied together like many phantom ships standing still in time and waiting for a call

From left to right: Sparky Pincus, Phil Baird from another LSM, and Ozzie Singer, storekeeper aboard a mine sweeper. This was taken at the Tropicana Night Club in Portland, OR, while we were all in the process of decommissioning our ships at Bremerton, Washington, after war's end.

to duty (or perhaps to the scrap heap). As it happened, both such things took place between 1946 and 1952.

In the meantime back aboard the 472, Captain Cyert asked me to get rid of some things that should not be aboard the ship while in storage. Among those were some electrical tools and the entire collection of V-Disc recordings that had been in my care as the disc jockey. I asked if I could keep them, and he said I should, so I sent the sixty-five 12" 78 rpm recordings back home. I loved that music and knew it was not available to the public and would never be available to me again. To this day, I still have them safely ensconced in my WWII museum, and they are played regularly on an old Fisher record player, probably one of the few 78 rpm's left in the world. To collectors (and me), they are priceless. As for the tools, they are still in my shop, and everyone today marvels at the simple and archaic fuse and circuit tester that works like a scale, with the needle registering the amount of voltage on a scale. It is a simple, but workable and effective, tool that I have had for almost sixty years. I guess the manufacturer during the war wanted to be sure it survived and did its good job for the navy.

I suppose that the final hour of our service aboard the 472 was with mixed emotions. We were all anxious to get discharged and go home, but we were leaving a crew we had bonded with and most likely would never see again. Of course, we were looking at old mother 472 for the last time as well. We had a big farewell party at the Tropicana Nightclub in Portland. As usual, my date brought a friend for the captain, and you can see what a wonderful time we had in the picture. I do not recall the captain's date's name, but I remember my date, Doris Jean Clark of Seattle, whom I met in the Western Union Telegraph office when we arrived from overseas and I was sending a telegraph to my folks to let them know I was home.

We finally got our orders to leave the ship, and I was to report to the Lido Beach Hotel in Lido Beach, Long Island, New York, for discharge. Lido was only a short ride from Bensonhurst, Brooklyn. Before I left the ship, my mentor and good friend, Lt. Cyert, sat me down and reminded me of my promise to go back to school if I survived. He also told me that if I wanted to

Back in the USA at a celebration of not only war's end, completion of the decommissioning of the old LSM-472. This took place at the Tropicana Night Club in Portland. Some of the men mentioned in this book are in the picture. First row from the left: Bennanatti, Junior Vaughn EM3/c, the author, Sparky Pincus, EM1/c Doris Jean Clark, Chuck Patterson, EM3/c. Next row from left: Captain, Lt. Richard M. Cyert and his blind date (arranged by the author and his date Doris Clark), gunner's mate Cannon and date, with Tex Texel BM1/c, Ensign Ed Breznack. Next row, standing from left: Eggert, ship's cook and friend, MM3/c B.H. Webb, Date, Bill Cooley and friend (he became a CIA agent after college), J. Moody, gunner's mate, Wild Man Deitz MM3/c, and date. Last row from left: Phil Baird from a sister ship, Paul Stevens and, finally, store-keeper 2/c, Jim Gorman. This was truly a wonderful evening and the end of our perilous journey.

stay in the Navy, because he knew how much I loved it, he had prepared for that possibility and had recommended me to Officers Candidate School. His last words to me were, "If you want to sign up for another four years, you will be an officer in a very short time, and you could make it your career." My reply was that I appreciated his thoughtfulness, but I had been away almost two years this trip and wanted to go home to see family and friends. He thought it was the right decision, he said, and hugged me and wished me well, as I did him. He asked me to keep in touch with him in Minneapolis, where he expected to be teaching. Saying goodbye to signalman Kearney, radioman Ed Rhoades, Josh Cope, and all the others that were like brothers by this time was particularly sad. I felt as though I had lived my whole life with them, and it was not easy parting ways.

The train ride home to New York was a long and tedious one, especially with the anticipation of seeing my family. I finally arrived, and two days later I was honorably discharged. I finally ended up on the Sea Beach Express subway that would take me to Avenue O, only one block from my parents' apartment. I got off the train and passed Pinky's Candy Store, which my folks had already sold, and as I walked up the steps to their apartment on the ground floor rear of the four-family brick house, with my sea bag, my Japanese Rifle, and Samurai sword, there was a large sign across the front door with the words "Welcome Home." It was truly the end of the war for me, and the end of the perilous journey as well.

There was a lot of hugging and kissing and shouting and laughing, except that my father was not present. Then I was told that he was quite sick with emphysema and was in the hospital. We cut the reunion short and went to visit him. He was happy to see me and paraded me around the hospital, introducing me to all the people he knew as a hero, which of course, I was not. I was his hero, however, so I indulged him. In reality, it was he who was my hero, having traveled all alone across Europe from Russia at age eighteen, ending up in England, where he worked as a coal stoker on a dirty tramp steamer to pay for his passage to America. He had no education and could not read or write English, but became a successful businessman in the roaring '20s with a fleet of 100 taxicabs.

Three days later, he passed away at the hospital, and, despite my loss, I was happy that I had come home and had seen him. I am grateful for that.

Chapter Ten

Civilian Life Once Again

W hen I was able to handle my grief and disappointment, I tried to turn my thoughts to Lt. Cyert and my promise to him, and I enrolled in Boro Hall Academy, a private high school, and spent my first summer finishing the 12th grade. I passed and received my diploma, moving on to Long Island University. After completing the university, I went to Brooklyn Law School. I had gone back to high school at age twenty-two and became an attorney at age twenty-five.

After passing the New York Bar Examination and being sworn in as an attorney-at-law, my friend from Brooklyn Law School and myself decided to celebrate our admission and went out to the 181 Club on Second Avenue in New York City. This was the "in" place to go and had a great review featuring singers, dancers, etc. As we waited in the lobby for our table, I noticed a poster-sized picture of the star of the show, whose name was Kit Russell. She was a beautiful blonde and quite successful in show business it seemed.

When we finally sat down at our table, we watched the review and especially enjoyed Kit Russell, who sang and danced. I kept saying that she looked familiar to me, but I could not place her. Suddenly, it dawned on me. She was not a she, but a "he," and her real name was Russell Paul. He had served aboard my first ship, the *USS Chaffee,* Destroyer Escort 230, as Yeoman 3rd Class. When I mentioned that to all the revelers at our table, they said I must be hallucinating, but I insisted I was right. I called the waitress over and gave her a tip so she would give Kit a note from me at the end of the show. I scribbled on the paper, "If you are really Russell Paul, Yeoman 3rd Class from the *USS Chaffee,* I am Al 'Sparky' Pincus, Electrician's Mate 1st Class, and I am in the audience."

After the show, "Kit" came flying out of the dressing room towards our table without the blonde wig, but still in women's clothes and makeup, grabbed me in a bear hug, and was indeed happy to see one of the crew from his old ship, some five years after the war had ended. My friends were stunned as Russell told us all about becoming a female impersonator, which was something he had always wanted to do. So I was vindicated, but, alas, none of us ever saw the famous Kit Russell again.

One of the first transactions I ever handled as an attorney was a real estate closing in New York City. On the way home, I stopped to get a newspaper in a Hallmark card shop, and who was behind the counter but Sal Amico, my old shipmate from the Bronx and the USS *Chaffee.* It was the second time we met by accident since we were both electrician's mates aboard the *Chaffee.* We renewed our friendship and met again after that day.

I never did find Lt. Cyert and finally gave up trying. It was not until I found Josh Cope in 1999 that I learned that Lt. Cyert had moved to Pittsburgh many years before to become a university professor.

I wished that I could have found him earlier to thank him for his guidance and inspiration. He truly did turn my life around, and I shall never forget him.

Now, in the twilight of my life, I look back at those wonderful shipmates and the memories we will forever share on that journey as a member of the greatest navy the world has ever known.

U.S. Navy Amphibious Forces – World War II

Printed in the USA
CPSIA information can be obtained
at www.ICGtesting.com
JSHW082357140824
68134JS00020B/2117